Rethinking Information Technology Asset Management

Rethinking Information Technology Asset Management

Jeremy L. Boerger

BUSINESS EXPERT PRESS

Leader in applied, concise business books

Rethinking Information Technology Asset Management

Copyright © Business Expert Press, LLC, 2021.

Cover design by Charlene Kronstedt

Interior design by Exeter Premedia Services Private Ltd., Chennai, India

First published in 2021 by
Business Expert Press, LLC
222 East 46th Street, New York, NY 10017
www.businessexpertpress.com

ISBN-13: 978-1-63742-014-0 (paperback)
ISBN-13: 978-1-63742-015-7 (e-book)

Business Expert Press Information Systems Collection

Collection ISSN: 2156-6577 (print)
Collection ISSN: 2156-6593 (electronic)

First edition: 2021

10 9 8 7 6 5 4 3 2 1

To Bob Menke:
You said I should, and I finally did
I wish you were here to see it

Description

Information technology asset management (ITAM) and software asset management (SAM) is hard. Annual IT budget forecasts rarely hold up for the entire year. There are plenty of excuses given:

- Untrustworthy reporting from the CMDB or MDR
- Unplanned version upgrades or platform refreshes
- Unapproved software, license, or cloud computing subscriptions coming due
- Unanticipated software license audit penalties
- And on, and on, and on

Rethinking Information Technology Asset Management presents a new answer to the problem. Most business leaders and IT managers assume nothing can be done. That these problems are part-and-parcel of modern IT. This book presents a new method—Pragmatic ITAM—that offers permanent solutions to the ignored, underpinning issues driving hardware and software cost overruns.

This book is intended for business leaders and IT executives who are tired of missed budget forecasts, unexpected software audit penalties, untrustworthy CMDB or Asset MDR reports, and idea that this is "just the way it is."

Keywords

information technology asset management; ITAM; software asset management; SAM; volume license agreement; VLA; software audit; software license position report; configuration management database; CMDB; managed data repository; MDR; pragmatic ITAM; budget; true up; renewal

Contents

Acknowledgments

If you are the kind of person to read the acknowledgements, then I hope you also don't mind the footnotes sprinkled throughout this book. They are there mostly for levity; to break up a rather dry subject.[1]

First, this book would not be possible without the help of Gillian Singletary. I am the architect and engineer of *Pragmatic ITAM*, but she is the general contractor, surveyor, carpenter, electrician, plumber, painter, and interior designer. I am no writer by any means, and she deftly accepted the herculean (or, better, Amazonian?) task of converting my dissonant scribbles, notes, slide decks, and recordings, into a proper book. Andrea Dale was so right to connect us to each other!

Second, the good folks at Business Expert Press deserve recognition for the opportunity to put my words to print. Scott Isenberg and Dan Power, Exeter team, producer Charlene Kronstedt, and marketer Sheri Dean, and host of others. Many thanks for seeing the value in my work, patiently guiding me through the publishing process, and putting up with my questions and delays.

Various colleagues and mentors have influenced me greatly in my twenty-plus years as an information technology asset manager. Steven Russman, the executive director of the IBSMA (International Business Software Managers Association), granted my first platform to discuss *Pragmatic ITAM* back at SAM Summit 2016. Sandi Conrad was there, and over red wine and chocolate-coated bacon, convinced me these ideas should be written down. Matthew Eversole, Linda Androvich, Rick Piatak, and Stephen Forrester, at various times in my career, took a chance on me and allowed me to learn, grow, experiment, test, and refine my

---

[1] I was inspired by the great Arthur C. Clark to use footnotes to converse with readers directly. In his Millennium series—*2001: A Space Odyssey, 2010: Odyssey Two, 2061: Odyssey Three,* and *3001: The Final Odyssey*—are peppered with footnotes talking about the real science behind the plot. Sometimes, the footnotes took up more of the page than the story itself!

craft with each iteration. But it was Bill Harley who started it all, way back in 1999.

I want to especially thank a small group of friends and cohorts who contributed greatly to the creation and refinement of this book's content. Robert Cherry, Matthew Curtiss, and Gladys Mason helped lay the groundwork of what would become the "Tenants of ITAM." Dr. John A. Lynch, III, offered timely insight and guidance in navigating non-fiction writing. Christopher Rismiller offered his entrepreneurial experience and know-how in starting my own consulting firm. And then Brian McKibben, who offered neither insight nor experience, but plenty of beer and encouragement when this project seemed to go on forever.

Then, to the rest of my family and friends: thank you for all the love and support you have shown me over the years. I would have never written a book without your blessings, and I could not have finished it without all of your encouragement. Stephen, Roger, and Ilsa—my children—this book doesn't make up for all the missed appointments, late arrivals, and time spent apart; I hope you can forgive me. It is just that all three of you make me so proud to be your father, and I want to accomplish something that would make you just as proud of me.

Finally, lastly, and most important of all, there is Lisa. My love, my darling, my brown-eyed girl.

CHAPTER 1

Introduction

The oldest documents to survive antiquity are Sumerian receipts estimated to be 7,000 years old. Written in cuneiform on clay tablets, this documentation has all of the recognizable details one would expect in a modern transfer of custody: who is making the purchase, who is recording it, what kind of stuff and how much, and so on.[1]

It takes little imagination to frame the scene: the scribe, reed stylus in hand (maybe a few spares tucked into his hair) dutifully recording the contents of the transaction, making small talk with the customer, the late summer sun high in the sky, a light breeze signaling autumn is approaching.

Truly, things have not changed much since. Swap that stylus and tablet for their electronic counterparts (no coincidence, they are also referred to as a stylus and tablet). Paper and ink crank out of a receipt printer on the counter—or are automatically sent via SMS to the purchaser—after money is exchanged. Our modern scribe is still recording the same data: who is making the purchase, who is recording it, what kind of clothing and how much, where the product originated, and so on.[2]

While the scene might be the same, modern technology has sped up the process. The ancient scribe would have needed to carefully bake his clay tablet to record his work, then filed it away in a document repository near the market for easy retrieval when the king's tax collectors came

---

[1] The record holder for the oldest-known receipt is actually for clothing. It currently resides in the British Museum collection of Mesopotamia artifacts. The British Museum also possesses the world's oldest complaint letter, regarding poor-quality copper ingots, and reads like every one-star Amazon or eBay review.

[2] Want more proof? The British Museum also possesses the world's oldest joke. It is mildly NSFW by today's standards, but variants are still told by middle school kids to this day.

to visit. Our modern scribe simply presses an onscreen button with her electronic stylus on her electronic tablet and all her work is instantly saved in a database for safekeeping. When the king's collectors ask to audit the market, our ancient scribe would retrieve the germane tablets, calculate all the incomes and outgoings, then produce another clay tablet with all of his notes and calculations. That might take a couple of days or even a week. His modern counterpart has her information and reports in seconds.

The steps to create that audit have not changed. Auditors sent not by the King but by software publishers still have the same requirements: documentation of resources used, sold, purchased. Technology has made it easier and faster than ever to collect that information, even automating many of the steps. Why, then, do modern Information Technology (IT) departments still fail so miserably at recording and tracking the disposition of their assets?

According to one survey from 2013, 52 percent of companies expect software audit penalties to exceed 10 percent of their revenue.[3] An IT Security survey from 2017 estimated that 47 percent of data breaches were caused by human error including "lost devices" and "not securing the device when away."[4] Such breaches are expected to generate costs between $1.1 to $3.8 million dollars per single incident.[5]

It's no surprise then that an entire industry has cropped up to help organizations get a grip on the problem. IT Asset Management (ITAM) and its subgroup Software Asset Management (SAM) will be valued at over U.S.$1.3 billion by 2024.[6]

What does all this mean? It means you, Technology Executive, are probably on the losing end of these numbers. If left unchecked, IT overspend

---

[3] "Tips to Get Ready for (or Possibly Avoid) Software Audits" by Rich Hein, CIO.com

[4] "The biggest cybersecurity risk to US businesses is employee negligence, study says" by Carmen Reinicke, CNBC.com

[5] "The cost of 2017 data breaches" by Dave Rickard, CSOOnline.com

[6] "IT Asset Management (ITAM) Software Market (Enterprise Size—SMEs, Large Enterprise; Deployment—On Premise, Cloud, Hybrid; End Use—BFSI, Telecom and IT, Government, Healthcare, Transportation, Manufacturing, Energy and Utilities)—Global Industry Analysis, Size, Share, Growth, Trends, and Forecast 2016–2024", August 2016.

and unbudgeted audit penalties will bleed your organization dry. In the most dire cases, this overspend can lead to layoffs, a chronic lack of IT resources, and the launch of a vicious cycle where your IT department can never catch up.

How to Use This Book

This book is intended to lay out the central tenets of the *Pragmatic ITAM* methodology. It's not an ITAM manual and it won't hold your hand through implementing ITAM in your business.

It will help you to:

- Come to grips with why your current ITAM program keeps failing
- Understand the asset lifecycle and why it's so critical in developing an effective ITAM program
- Develop the underlying infrastructure necessary to launch a successful ITAM program
- Learn what it means for your asset data to be inarguably accurate and be prepared to weaponize that data in the case of a software license audit
- Identify the right people to place on your ITAM team, and how to help them succeed

You'll be able to use this book not only as an introduction to my methodology but also as a reference when the time comes to manage, troubleshoot, and leverage your ITAM data.

Why This Book Is Necessary

This book is for the IT executive who is not an ITAM expert but who knows that their business needs to be doing a better job of managing its technology assets, including hardware and software.

Pragmatic ITAM is not the first ITAM methodology or resource available to technology executives or ITAM professionals. But after decades of working in this arena, it became impossible for me to ignore the limitations of these existing resources. Broadly speaking, the resources out there will tell you and your team what's required of an effective ITAM program but they won't help you figure out how to meet those requirements.

That's the gap that I'm aiming to fill with *Pragmatic ITAM*.

The two most commonly referred to resources in ITAM are ITIL and ISO/IEC 19770.

Pragmatic ITAM is designed to augment, support, and realize the full potential of ITIL and 19770, not replace them.

ITIL

Version 4 of the Information Technology Infrastructure Library (ITILv4) was released in 2019. Previous iterations of this body of knowledge gave only a passing mention or recognition to ITAM and SAM as a discipline, but never provided any real guidance or advice on hardware and software assets. This book seeks to resolve this oversight by detailing how ITAM and specifically SAM and SAM tools can help businesses meet their cost-savings goals by optimizing IT resources usage.

ISO/IEC 19770

Even broader than ITIL, the ISO (the International Organization for Standardization) and IEC (the International Electrotechnical Commission) create worldwide standardization guidelines for technology and beyond. ISO/IEC 19770 is the set of standardization guidelines that apply directly to ITAM.

As of 2017, the ISO/IEC guidelines are based around the idea of three total tiers of ITAM program sophistication:

1. Trustworthy Data: Essentially, this means being able to confirm that what you know about your computing environment is accurate.
2. Lifecycle Integration: Once you have established a level of trustworthy data, it is expected that you can move on to applying lifecycle tags to your assets, to realize "greater efficiency and cost-effectiveness."[7]
3. Optimization: Finally, these standards outline that an ITAM program with trustworthy data and lifecycle integration will be able to leverage

---

[7] ISO/IEC 19770-1, Third Edition.

their data repository for business advantage (e.g., moving assets through the lifecycle more quickly, recovering and reusing hardware assets and software licenses efficiently, etc.)

Each tier builds on the one before it. As you go through this book, you will be able to see how the *Pragmatic ITAM* methodology is set up to help you achieve each tier that's set forth by these standards.

How *Pragmatic* ITAM Is Different

One of the differences between *Pragmatic ITAM* and other methodologies is that it can act as an early warning system for your ITAM failures. *Pragmatic ITAM* is designed to help you instantly see the gaps in your knowledge, show you why these particular areas are failing (or on the way there) and prescribe the best way to fix your shortfalls. With the right implementation, it can do this way before an auditor comes along and wants to charge you for those shortfalls.

With the right ITAM approach, there is an opportunity to align technology needs with overall business goals—and that opportunity is already in your budget. I want to help you leverage that opportunity.

Here's what I know to be true:

1. Most ITAM initiatives fail because they are overwhelmed by the sheer amount of data coming into the program
2. Most corporations fail their software audits because they know less about their computing environment than the software publishers do
3. Most configuration management databases (CMDBs) and asset managed data repositories (MDRs) fail to keep up with modern corporate networks because they rely too much on manual interventions

You don't have to be "most" people. You can do better.

Tenets of *Pragmatic* ITAM

The rest of the book will show you exactly what *Pragmatic ITAM* looks like in practice, but I want to take this chance to outline the central tenets of the methodology.

1. Knowledge of the problem inherently changes the nature of the problem
2. She with the best documentation wins
3. Work smarter, not harder
4. Trust, but verify
5. Asset lifecycle management requires rigor
6. Process is a means to an end, and is not an end itself

These principles will come up with every step of the process and form a foundation for *Pragmatic ITAM*. It will be helpful to keep these ideas in the back of your mind as you implement the methodology.

Who Am I?

Like all good technology consultants, I graduated from the University of Dayton with a degree in Philosophy and History.

When being a stand-up philosopher[8] didn't work out, I found my way into IT and have worked in that sector for more than 20 years, with the last 20 in IT Asset Management. I have ITIL certifications including OSA, PPO, and RCV, and extensive experience in the manufacturing, financial, and healthcare sectors.

I founded Boerger Consulting to promote effective ITAM and SAM strategies for all organizations.

People in your position are getting punished every day for things like audit penalties and license overcharges that aren't really your fault. But you're not alone. *Pragmatic ITAM* can help.

---

[8] Clerk: Occupation?
Comicus: Stand-up Philosopher
Clerk: What?
Comicus: Stand-up philosopher. I coalesce the vapors of human experience into a viable and meaningful comprehension.
Clerk: Oh, a BS artist.
History of the World, Part 1 (1981)

CHAPTER 2

The Philosophy of ITAM

The genesis of *Pragmatic ITAM* arises from the struggles information technology asset managers have with organizing, tracking, and managing their hardware and software assets. Nearly every technology executive has a wealth of knowledge about what their business needs in order to be technologically efficient. But when I start to probe into their current ITAM practices (if they have any at all), I usually uncover little more than a vague notion that they "could be doing better."

This isn't an intellectual failing or a lack of motivation—although a lack of time and resources is often on the list of excuses.

Rather, I posit the problem stems not from a lack on the part of technology departments, asset managers, or executives but from a lack within the current asset management frameworks. In other words, it's not your fault.

What you will begin to appreciate in this chapter is, as it exists now, ITAM offers no methodology that compiles data in a way that is effective, comprehensive, and trends toward complete. That's precisely the inspiration behind my *Pragmatic ITAM* methodology. I knew that ITAM, as an industry, could also be doing better.

As I already noted, human beings have been performing asset management for millennia. With this kind of history on our side, why do we struggle when we attempt to apply these activities to the 21st century software and hardware assets?

As I have developed this methodology over my career, it has always struck me that so many consultants talk about asset management as if it is a fully-formed, regimented process. As if we can somehow discern the exact right sequence of numbers to punch into our tracking software, so it will spit out a complete report of trustworthy data.

This is simply not the case.

Effective ITAM means methodically uncovering more and more information to get a clear picture of your asset landscape. It's not about knowing how to type in the right numbers or where to find the keys to the supply closet, it's about developing an understanding of what you know, how you know it, and whether you can actually *confirm* that which you know is true.

By the end of this book, if you and your team follow the *Pragmatic ITAM* approach, you will have the trustworthy data you need for ISO/ IEC. Your license counters and inventories will be rock solid and inarguable. This verifiably accurate data will act as an early warning system. You know what assets you have with certainty, so when something goes wrong or goes missing, you will know much sooner and you will be able to investigate long before an audit occurs.

Verifiably accurate data gives you the confidence that your data is trustworthy, which means it can be accurately measured, recorded, proven, and no one—not vendor auditors, not drive-by managers, not know-it-all consultants—can argue with it.

If all that sounds a bit philosophical, that's because it is. In fact, *Pragmatic ITAM's* effectiveness comes from its foundations in classic philosophy. But before we dive into the philosophical foundations of the *Pragmatic ITAM* methodology, let's take a step back and look at how most ITAM processes are currently performed.

Transactional ITAM Versus Accountancy ITAM

There are two existing basic ITAM methodologies: transactional and accountancy.

Transactional ITAM

Transactional ITAM relies on interaction between users, departments, or companies to determine the status of an asset. For instance, an invoice is generated to document that money has changed hands from one corporation to another and that the purchased assets have come under the buyer's control. Then, a request or work order is generated to move the asset around to different areas within its new environment. A chain-of-custody certificate will denote where the owner's responsibility for the asset ends and becomes someone else's problem. If all goes according to process, any asset's location can be determined by simply researching the paper trail, be it laptop, program, or donut.[1]

But any asset manager knows that's one big IF. It's all too easy for an asset to move from one department to another with no paper trail, or for a receipt to turn up missing. But a lack of a receipt doesn't mean the asset doesn't exist. And you can probably imagine the added complexities that come along with assets that aren't physically observable, like software. IT departments around the world give into user requests for the latest software because they see their co-worker using it or need it for a single presentation. Do they generate a receipt or a work order or any documentation at all?

Maybe.

But probably not.

And what about coming into an organization that has no ITAM process in place and trying to start with this method. How old is the laptop sitting in the closet that hasn't been used in the last 12 months? And where's the receipt?

You can see the limitations here.

There is value in having a paper trail, but it can't be the only thing you're relying on in your ITAM process.

Let's look at another method.

Accountancy ITAM

The accountancy methodology follows the flow of monies as a representation of the assets being consumed by the corporation's department cost centers. It works like this: when setting a new budget, someone will perform an internal inventory to verify what equipment is in use by each department, what needs replacing, and if any other changes

---

[1] The late Mitch Hedberg joked, "I bought a donut and they gave me a receipt for the donut. I don't need a receipt for a donut. I'll just give you the money and you'll give me the donut. End of transaction! We don't need to bring ink and paper into this. I just could not imagine a scenario where I'd have to prove that I bought a donut. Some skeptical friend? 'Don't even act like I didn't get that donut! I got the documentation right here! Oh wait, it's back home... in the file... under 'D'... for donut.'"

have taken place that might require changes to the existing budget. If a question arises, like a budget overrun or external audit demand, another inventory is taken, compared to the first one, and the auditors try to explain away the differences.

Asset managers using the accountancy method strive to be accurate, but it's not hard to see how this methodology, too, lacks corroborating evidence to ensure its accuracy. If there is a discrepancy between one inventory and the next, who is to say which is actually accurate? Most accounting departments will not even bother, and just write off the difference as a loss.

Now you understand why ITAM has such a poor reputation for accuracy and usefulness.

If ITAM has all the transaction receipts, then it should be able to report on the state and disposition of each asset accurately.

If ITAM is taking inventory on a regular basis, then hardware and software budgets should be accurate year-over-year.

Technology exists to automate both the ticketing and inventory systems, and yet...

...hardware still gets lost,

...software still gets installed without buying it,

...and publishers and auditors still win at audits.

Both methodologies fail in a lack of verification.

When the transaction records are collated or the inventory finishes, an asset report is dropped on the CIO's desk with a thud. If anyone bothers to ask "how can you be sure?" or "is this really accurate?"—they're usually met with a shrug. These are the numbers and numbers don't lie.[2] End of story.

When those numbers turn out to be inaccurate, because of a closet missed during inventory, an unreported software installation, or myriad other reasons, that shrug turns seamlessly into a promise to do better next time.

Unfortunately, a shrug and a promise is less than effective at quelling the bloodthirsty auditors that are ready to pounce on any inaccuracy and demand a huge check in return for this casual carelessness.

Rather than fully formed methodologies, both transactional and inventory data are only the beginning of the process of managing all the

---

[2] My writer, Gillian, suggested a mention to Shakira's "Hips Don't Lie." My first thought was "Would I Lie To You?" by The Eurythmics. Can you detect the generational gap between us?

devices, programs, and services within the computing environment. The ITAM team needs to apply a rigorous, rational, and reasonable examination of the data to prove it accurate, inscrutable, and therefore, trustworthy. The rest of this book will deal with how that will be accomplished. This chapter is dedicated to the why.

What Is Epistemology?

Epistemology is a subset of general philosophy dedicated to the study of human knowledge. Where the word philosophy roughly translates to "a love of knowledge," epistemology finds its roots in the Greek words for "study of" (just like other sciences of biology, physiology, etc.) and "knowing." Epistemology looks to the nature and meaning of what knowledge is, how something is proven true or false, and the different ways facts and data can be organized.

Epistemology, in one form or another, has been around since the beginning of civilization. Over the years, it has branched into a number of interesting schools of thought, like empiricism, constructivism, and pragmatism. Its impact can be seen in everything from statistical analysis, particle physics, quantum mechanics, and artificial intelligence. *Pragmatic ITAM* started from an observation that IT asset management is tasked to answer similar questions as these other modern studies: what do we know and how well do we know it?

The rest of this chapter is going to take a deeper dive into a couple of lessons from three famous epistemology philosophers: Socrates, Pascal, and Descartes.[3] The rest of this book will demonstrate how these ideas

---

[3] The three philosophers cited are admittedly part of the "old, dead, white guy" pantheon. Epistemology is a universally human endeavor, with some amazing contributions from all over the world. The ninth century philosopher Abu ʿAli al-Husayn ibn Sina (also known as Avicenna) should also be recognized for his continuing influence. Hinduism and Buddhism both have long and storied histories of epistemological thought. And, if this were a proper philosophy textbook (or if I were a better-read philosopher), there would be whole chapters devoted to female, LGBTQ, and POC writers. After reading this book, if you are interested in learning more about philosophy for fun (hey, you're my kinda person), I encourage you to seek out a broader representation than I have been able to include.

anchor *Pragmatic ITAM* to a sound methodology that will result in trustworthy CMDB and Asset MDRs.

Socrates and the Allegory of the Cave

Socrates, featured here in Figure 2.1, lived in Ancient Greece, sometime between 470 to 399 BCE. While many philosophers and historians point to him as the originator of Western philosophy, few of his original works survive. Almost all of our knowledge about him and his views comes from his contemporaries and students, the most famous being Plato.

In Plato's *The Republic*, we find Socrates and his students at a dinner party. Socrates uses the gathering to touch on a wide breadth of subjects, including ethics, politics, leadership, and the nature of human knowledge.

Figure 2.1 Socrates (469–399 BCE) on engraving from 1788. Classical Greek Athenian philosopher. Considered one of the founders of Western philosophy. Engraved by T. Trotter after Peter Paul Rubens and published in Essays on Physiognomy, UK, 1788

Socrates begins with an allegory, asking his compatriots to imagine themselves as a prisoner, shackled to a cave wall. Up and behind, there is a single light source that casts shadows on a wall in front of you. These shadows are made by people and things passing along a causeway, but your restraints prevent you from observing this directly. Instead, your entire understanding of what is going on is limited to only images cast on the wall in front of you.

Socrates then opens the floor to his fellow party guests. All admit that this sort of existence is not ideal, to say the least. But Socrates also gets them to admit that these prisoners can still form a fairly accurate understanding of their world in spite of their limited field of view. The prisoners should be able to know what people look like; what a cart looks like; maybe even suss out the meaning and purpose of objects and goods being carried along the causeway.

Socrates continues his analogy by imagining the prisoner's escape. You slip your shackles, scramble up over the wall behind you, and make your way to the causeway. At this point, you get your first direct look at the people and objects you first came to know as passing shadows. You are still in the cave, so your vision is hampered by the meager light that cast the shadows in the first place. But your situation has certainly improved, and you are now in a position to make new observations about the people and objects on the causeway. How, Socrates asks, will that change your understanding? Will you hold onto the preconceived notions you formed from the shadows before? Or will you replace them with the improved perceptions you have now?

Socrates finishes the analogy by letting the prisoner go free into the outside world. Now under full daylight, our senses see the world as it is. What will our freed prisoner make of his initial notions and observations from within the cave? Or even the causeway? Socrates makes two conclusions:

1. Our understanding of the world around us is limited by our ability to observe and experience it.
2. Obtaining true understanding of the world is a process that requires recognition of our initial observational limitations and that we seek ways to overcome these biases with new information and new observations.

Truly, this is a good life lesson.

But how does it apply to IT asset management?

Let's start with the second conclusion: true understanding is a process that takes time.

- No ITAM tool or team will be able to provide all the answers to all the questions at the moment of installation. ITAM takes time. Just as our prisoner in his cave had to build upon his initial shadowy understanding of the world day by day, so too do asset managers need to leave the cave of their discovery tools to build on what they think they know at any given moment.

- Discovery tools need time to scan the corporate computing environment, return that information to the central database, and then to make sense of it. Even as he gained more and more access to the world around him, our prisoner surely had to take time to process how each physical object or human being related back to the shadows he had first seen.

- ITAM team members need time to conduct research, find the appropriate knowledge holders, locate the proper underpinning documentation, and organize all that information into a catalog that makes sense. Our prisoner had to go out beyond the causeway and explore the world before he had a full understanding of what he was seeing on his first day in the cave.

Pragmatic ITAM will be crafting metrics and key performance indicators (KPIs) that describe a similar journey as Socrates's prisoner. These measures will aim to show that what is known about the computing environment at the start of the ITAM process will be expanded on and replaced with new information as it comes to light. And there's no requirement that you chain yourself in a cave to make this methodology work.

Back to the first conclusion: consider the type and quality of the information presented to our prisoner. At the beginning of the analogy, the prisoner can only visually observe at a distance. The prisoner cannot touch the shadows on the far wall. Presume the prisoner can hear—but what kind of information will muffled echoes present? To say nothing of musty cave smells.

Upon his escape, both the quantity and quality of the information presented to the prisoner improves. In the same way, *Pragmatic ITAM* must also fashion KPIs to measure and track the improvements of the environmental data over time, thereby demonstrating its impact to the rest of the IT department's operations and expenditures.

If you know you could and should be doing a better job of IT asset management, take comfort in the fact that what your team knows now is not the same as what they will know tomorrow or next week. Just as our prisoner friend could eventually trace shadow to person, so too will your asset managers be able to trace receipt, to serial number, to physical asset. Your body of knowledge will build over time and increasingly be able to reflect reality.

René Descartes and Categorical Doubt

René Descartes (pictured in Figure 2.2) made significant contributions to the fields of science, philosophy, mathematics, physics, anatomy, military strategy, and ethics that are still in use to this day. He is literally a Renaissance man: his book, *Meditations on First Philosophy*, marks the boundary between the Middle Ages and the European Renaissance in the 17th century.

In *Meditations*, Descartes sets out an ambitious goal: to "restart" human philosophy by removing all the assumptions and preconceived notions, rebuilding it on a solid foundation of reason and logic. On this journey of what will become known as categorical doubt, he tackles one of the most fundamental questions in philosophy: how does one go about proving one's own existence? To begin, he goes after the underlying question: what is the true nature of reality?

Descartes was well-versed in anatomy and physiology and knew humans perceive the world through their senses. The mind does not experience reality directly but indirectly, meaning there is the possibility of a disconnect between what the mind perceives as reality and what is *actually* real. Descartes concludes there are three scenarios that could cause such a disconnect:

1. **He's Dreaming.** It could be that what Descartes is experiencing as reality is, proverbially, all in his head. At some point in the future, he

Figure 2.2 Rene Descartes (1596–1650 BCE) on engraving from the 1800s. French philosopher, mathematician, physicist and writer. Engraved by W. Holl and published in London by Wm. S. Orr & Co

could wake up and reality could be completely different from what he is accustomed to.

2. **He's Wrong.** The possibility exists that reality is correct, but Descartes's perception is not. Somewhere after sensing the world and before his mind perceives the information, something goes haywire. What feels cold is actually hot. What tastes sweet is actually sour. What looks red is actually blue. And so on.

3. **He's Enthralled.** What if the senses are working correctly and the mind is interpreting those senses correctly but something (or someone) is forcing his mind to perceive hot as cold, sour as sweet, blue as red? Descartes imagined an "evil genius" hijacking his mind and forcing associations between his perceptions and his reality.[4]

---

[4] Does any of this sound familiar? It should. Modern writers and directors have turned these scenarios into popular science fiction tropes. This author's favorite is *The Matrix (1999)*.

But just when you think he has deductively boxed himself into a corner, Descartes points out that all three scenarios have a common denominator: his mind. Regardless if the world is real or just a dream, regardless if his senses are accurate or not, or if he's under an evil genius's spell, his mind is being acted upon. This leads him to one of the most profound existential statements in Western philosophy: *cogito, ergo sum*. In English: *I think, therefore I am*.

Coming back to the purpose of this book: how does this realization help with IT asset management? ITAM's purpose is to accurately describe and track all the information technology hardware and software assets that make up a corporate computing environment. Descartes presents us with two strategies for determining whether something is actually part of that environment or not.

The first is the concept of categorical doubt, which asks us to assume all data is suspect unless we can prove it to be accurate. Descartes only began his process of philosophical discovery because he decided to assume that perhaps everything he already knew was based on a false premise. Indeed, this is where IT asset management must begin. No data should be recorded onto a configuration item or asset record unless it comes from a verified source. *Pragmatic ITAM's* goal will be to find ways to confirm data before it is entered into the CMDB.

The second relates to the nature of existence. Descartes realized he exists because things are happening to his mind and the same can be said for devices on a computer network:

- If a device is assigned an IP address (as in, internet protocol address) by the DHCP system (or, rather, the Domain Host Configuration Protocol system), then it must have existed on the network at some point in time because the DHCP system was able to make a log entry for it.
- If a serial number appears on a visual inventory report, then at the time it was notated on the report, that device existed in the depot.
- Underpinning documents with serial number and date information such as bills of lading (incoming) or certificates of destruction (outgoing) are also evidence that at one point in time, a specific device was part of the corporate computing environment.

Where Socrates lets us paint a more and more accurate picture as we learn more about the reality of our environment, Descartes shows us how the way things (in our case, assets) interact can give us another layer of certainty as to the accuracy of our data.

Blaise Pascal and Pascal's Wager

Blaise Pascal (who's portrait is Figure 2.3) was a contemporary of René Descartes during the dawn of the Renaissance. He was considered a child prodigy, making significant contributions to science, analytical geometry, economics, ethics, and theology very early in his life. Unfortunately, his poor health cut his life short at the age of 39, leaving many of his efforts incomplete and unpublished.

Figure 2.3 Blaise Pascal (1623–1662 BCE) on engraving from the 1800s. French mathematician, physicist, and religious philosopher. Engraved by H. Meyer and published in London by Charles Knight, Pall Mall East

Some of Pascal's notes for a book on ethics were published posthumously as *Pensées* (in English, *Thoughts*). It is in this work that we find a discussion now known as "Pascal's Wager." In it, Pascal attempts to create a mathematical model to explain why someone should live a religious life. He argues there are two related and bivalent questions:

1. Is there, factually, an afterlife?
2. And, have you, actually, lived a religious life with all the sacrifices and efforts such requires?

According to Pascal, both of these questions can only be answered "yes" or "no" (i.e., bivalent). These questions are also related; both must be answered to achieve a predicted outcome. The desirable outcome for Pascal is to reach Paradise and the infinite rewards promised by the religious thought of his time. The undesirable destination is infinitely worse. But if there is no afterlife, then living with all the religiously devoted sacrifices doesn't matter either way. Pascal concludes that it is better to assume an afterlife exists and live your life so that your soul qualifies for Paradise than to be wrong and punished with eternal hellfire and brimstone.

It can be confusing, so let's examine the chart in Figure 2.4. Both questions are represented along the axes. Each row and column represents the bivalent answer to each question. The four quadrants display the cost and benefit of each potential outcome.

Pascal's Wager			
		Is there are afterlife?	
		NO	YES
Do I live religiously?	YES	Some cost :: No reward	Some cost :: Infinite reward!
	NO	No cost :: No reward	No cost :: Infinite punishment!

Figure 2.4 *A simple decision matrix, detailing the risk reward ratios emergent from the bivalent questions presented*

It should now become clearer what Pascal was wagering for. The return on the cost of living a religious life is infinitely more desirable than betting wrong. And if it turns out that there is no Paradise after death, are you really out that much?

This chart should also look familiar to anyone who has done modern SWOT analysis (strength, weakness, opportunity, threat), or leveraged an Eisenhower time-management system. *Pragmatic ITAM* will use it to highlight which asset populations present the most risk and require more effort to resolve.

Conclusion

Pragmatic ITAM will be resolving a number of the current hardware and software asset management practices by grounding itself in an epistemological approach. The following lessons from the great minds of Western philosophy will be continually referenced and recalled throughout the book:

- Understanding an organization's computing environment requires a number of different measures to complete the whole picture.
- Over time, we should expect our understanding to change as new information and details are revealed through our research efforts.
- Items that make up the computing environment will be confirmed by how they interact with each other.
- Do not assume a data source to be correct, devise ways to confirm it with more data.
- Leverage logical tests of the data, á la Pascal's Wager, to predict and confirm the ITAM team's efforts are having a positive effect.

IT gets expensive when things break and you have to drop everything you are doing to go fix it. In ITAM, things "break" when someone drops a license audit on you: it's going to get expensive, and you have to devote resources to it that would be doing something else. *Pragmatic ITAM* allows you to spot these issues early and address them so you won't have to fear the auditor.

CHAPTER 3

Starting Pragmatic ITAM: Phase one

Discovery Source Alignment

Nearly every IT asset management project starts with a messy dataset and a lot of unknowns. With the right methodology, your ITAM team can turn even the ugliest data into a thing of beauty and keep it that way. Information about your IT assets will be verifiably accurate and inarguable, even by the most aggressive auditor.

That's our goal with *Pragmatic ITAM*.

We'd all love to start at the end, with ironclad data and a fully realized ITAM report, but we also know that's far from realistic. *Pragmatic ITAM* takes the advice of Vizzini, and goes back to the beginning: we start with discovery.[1]

By the end of this section, you will learn:

- The best practices for selecting the data sources your ITAM team can use to get a clear and approaching complete picture of your entire computing environment
- How best to view and present those data sources
- How to assess your discovery to determine its accuracy with relevant critical success factors and key performance indicators

---

[1] "I am waiting for you, Vizzini. You told me to go back to the beginning. So I have. This is where I am, and this is where I'll stay. I will not be moved... When a job went wrong, you went back to the beginning. And this is where we got the job. So it's the beginning, and I'm staying till Vizzini comes." Inigo Montoya, *The Princess Bride* (1987).

Phase One: Discovery Source Alignment

Pragmatic ITAM is about knowing what you know and understanding what you don't know. Since you cannot prove a negative, let's start by figuring out what you know.

We call that discovery.

Epistemology directs us to scrutinize all the data coming into a system. While that sounds extreme, it actually simplifies things. It doesn't matter if we are starting with an existing asset management dataset or a brand new CMDB: all of our data sources should be treated as suspect until we can verify them.

Until you have a robust ITAM process in place, it's foolhardy to assume that any data you already have is accurate or complete. Imagine if we had done that in Socrates' cave. The *Pragmatic ITAM* methodology aims to remove assumptions from the equation entirely by starting from square one. When you know for certain what you know and it's verifiably accurate, you put yourself and your company in the strongest possible position whether you're facing down a vendor audit or a budget crisis.

Discovery information can be classified into three different categories:

1. **Electronic Inventory** (EI), data about the environment from the devices themselves, collected into a remote database or repository
2. **Visual Inventory** (VI), what human individuals can witness and attest to as they move through the environment
3. **Underpinning Documentation**, the written records, receipts, contracts, and so on, associated with an asset inventory that provides a legal or procedural foundation of data

Electronic Inventory

Electronic evidence is the easiest place to start gathering environmental data. Modern IT computing environments have a number of different remote monitoring and management tools that possess a wealth of information about what is going on in those environments. These "command and control" tools use two strategies to harvest data from the network: deploying agents to computers and passively scanning the environment.

Deployed Agent

A deployed agent or local agent scanning tool is a small program that runs in the background of a computer's operating system. These scanning tools collect data from the computer and transmit it to a centralized server. These scans can also be scheduled, which has the advantage of not taking up computing bandwidth during peak hours.

One drawback of this strategy is that if the program is disabled for any reason, the machine will seem to have disappeared from the network and will not be reported, but we can actually use this to our advantage. When an asset is supposed to be there and stops being there, that's a piece of data that should trigger action from your asset manager. Uncovering this type of actionable data is exactly the point of the discovery process. The more robust your ITAM program, the quicker you will find these actionable nuggets and the more automatic the necessary correlating actions will become.

Agentless Scan

An agentless scan or remote scanning tool runs on a network without needing to be installed on any individual computer. The tool sends out a general broadcast signal across a range of IP addresses, and listens for a response. When a computer responds, the scanning tool sends a list of automated commands and the computer returns the requested details about itself. When a new machine is added, not much may be known about it, but the agentless tool will at minimum report its existence.

An agentless scan can bog down a network because multiple scans are needed to collect all the expected data. Furthermore, if the timing of the scan is misaligned with the working hours of the device, the tool will never pick up the data because the computer is never there to respond.[2]

Worse, some devices don't like to be pinged. For instance, medical devices—remote telemetry, IV pumps, dialysis systems—are notoriously resistant to remote scanning and can cause "negative patient impact events" if scanned.

---

[2] "Bueller? Bueller? Bueller?", Economics Teacher, played by Ben Stein, in *Ferris Bueller's Day Off* (1986)

Pragmatic ITAM, therefore, recommends deployed agents. No matter which one is in use, these tools can harvest many details on many systems in a very short amount of time, often without human intervention.

More often than not, these scanning tools do not pass information back and forth to each other. Each usually has a specific job at its core: to control data access, to deploy software and security patches, to alert administrators to issues and threats, and the like. This lack of cross-functionality prompted the development of configuration management databases and managed data repositories in the first place. The larger CMDBs and Asset MDRs on the market usually include their own data harvesting tools to get around the cumbersome and unreliable process of pulling data from external systems.

Visual Inspection

It isn't technologically sophisticated and there's no software to buy (or sell), but the fact remains that when you want a complete inventory of your IT assets, nothing beats a good set of eyes. Scanning tools can go on for days pinging IP addresses with no results. Every good ITAM manager has a horror story about finding a closet full of unaccounted for laptops or servers that were never deployed. At some point, ITAM teams must be prepared to get out their magnifying glasses and pound the pavement looking for physical, visual clues as to what assets are really in your inventory.[3]

The trouble with visual inspections is twofold. First, they are time consuming and disruptive. ITAM team members tasked with taking a visual inspection will not be able to do much else while they're in the field. Worse, they'll need access to secured spaces, scheduled visits to remote locations, travel, escorts through production facilities, and so on. That means, they will need to engage other teams (and take up their time) to grant the access, prepare for the visits, and walk the ITAM team safely through the production areas.

---

[3] Those server closets would've gotten away with it, too, if it weren't for your meddling ITAM team! (A nod to *Scooby-Doo, Where Are You!* [1969]).

Second, visual inventory results will be immediately obsolete the second they are recorded. Why? Modern businesses, and the computing environments that support them, are dynamic places. As soon as an ITAM team member turns her back and marks a device as present in the storage depot, a service manager could swoop in and deploy it. That visual inspection record is now wrong: said device is no longer in storage, but now deployed.

Luckily, an IT department has other ways to visually confirm which assets are in use on the network. Think about how most people in an organization interact with IT: through the help desk. Every time someone goes out to repair a machine or has a misbehaving laptop unceremoniously dropped on their desk is an opportunity to visually confirm its existence as well as what programs are installed. In this way, Incident Management and Asset Management can work together to get a better picture of what's happening in the computing environment.

Underpinning Documentation

Underpinning documentation is more than just the paper detritus generated by organizations doing business. Think of it as the physical manifestation of the comings and goings of the goods, services, and monies flowing in and out of the organization. This is doubly so for nonphysical concepts like intellectual property, use licenses, and service agreements.

The best underpinning documents will have a few key features: names of the parties involved, descriptions of the goods, services, dollars, et cetera, moving between them, and a date.

The date stamp will be most key because it lets us assign an exact date to an explicit stage of the asset lifecycle. We will get into why this is so important (and cover a lot more on the asset lifecycle) in later chapters.

The most common documents ITAM teams deal with include purchase orders (POs) and invoices, bills of lading (BoLs) and certificates of disposal (CoDs). This documentation is not always so easy to identify or find. In some cases, you might be lucky and have a highly organized receiving department with perfectly tabbed binders of BoLs. In other cases, ITAM teams might have to use all their powers of persuasion and persistence to get a forward of an e-mail chain about when an asset was first purchased, installed, or destroyed. It can be a crapshoot, but this documentation is essential because it shows, as of the date printed on the paperwork, that the device should be (or no longer will be) found by EI or VI efforts.

Transforming "Discovery" Into "Trustworthy Data"

We now have a treasure trove of wonderful data in front of us: electronic inventory from our scanning tools, visual inspections from our sites, and underpinning documents from our archives. Now the danger lies in analysis paralysis: we have so much data to organize and interpret, we get overwhelmed and distracted from delivering results.

We need guidelines that can help us categorize and prioritize which data goes into our CMDB. That's where Primacy of Evidence comes in.

Primacy of Evidence

The term Primacy of Evidence comes to us by way of American and British criminal law. The core idea is that witness testimony and observation (i.e., data) closest to the loci and time of the event (i.e., that which is being investigated) holds more weight (i.e., has primacy) than data collected farther from that loci and time, like what a nonwitness *hears* someone *say* about the event.[4]

The best example is the children's game Telephone, where a line of kids whispers a phrase from one to the next, until the last child reports to the group what she heard. Hilarity ensues, because whatever the last child hears is certainly not the phrase the first kid whispered. The first kid, who chose the phrase to start the game, knows what she said. She has primacy. Every child in line to the last will have a lesser degree of primacy until you reach the last child in line.

Think back to Socrates and the cave analogy. Those shadows cast on the wall are indirect projections. They have lower primacy of evidence compared to examining the items directly by torchlight. And that evidence is lesser than witnessing reality in all its sun-bathed glory outside the cave.

---

[4] This is the origin of the word "hearsay," which TV lawyers love to say.

But we should be careful not to apply a blanket primacy assessment to an entire source.

Certain details presented within a source could have varying degrees of primacy compared to others. For instance, one underpinning document could possess certain facts with a high degree of primacy, while other facts presented in that same document might have a higher primacy from a different document. Think to the interplay between contracts and amendments, where the amendment wording will have a higher primacy than the preceding language in the original contract document[5].

Consider our ancient Sumerian scribe, dutifully recording grain deposits. His notes on how many bushels of grain were delivered to the granary on a specific date should be considered high primacy of evidence. He is probably counting up the bushels himself before the oxcart is unloaded and recording his own observations. But what of his other notes? How does he know where the grain originated? He wasn't out in the field observing harvest—he's busy enough at the granary. Our scribe probably wrote down what he was told by the person making the delivery. And how would the delivery man know? Maybe he was with the cart when the farmers loaded it in the field? Or maybe he's just a middleman passing information from the original sender down the line? Either way, just because it was written down by our dutiful scribe does not mean it should carry the same evidentiary weight, as details we know the scribe himself to have observed.

Back in our modern IT computing environment, how is this helpful?

Remember, we're attempting to measure the computing environment itself. And what makes up the computing environment? The component laptops, desktops, servers, switches, and so on, operating within it.

---

[5] There is a troubling trend, especially with SaaS and cloud computing licensing agreements, to "store" Terms & Conditions and license definitions online, then mention the URL to those documentations within the contract. SaaS and cloud service providers then sneak in a provision in the main body of the contract to allow them to change the wording on these stored documents at their leisure and benefit, and even without notification, while still holding the licensee accountable to the new terms. A good SAM manager will keep their eyes open for such legal shenanigans!

Therefore, any data coming from those components themselves should be considered to have a high primacy of evidence.

The unfortunate reality is that the multiple electronic discovery tools available may or may not communicate with one another. That means, the ITAM team has multiple electronic data sources to choose from, but no good starting point. Best business practices would tell us to declare one source as the "record of note" or "source of truth" but how do we go about choosing that source?

Not every source will be optimal for every platform or location. One tool might only work on a particular operating system. Another will only gather software installation details and miss other data necessary for critical license position calculations. Choosing your own source of truth will depend exclusively on the quirks and particulars of your environment.

Beyond electronic inventory, visual inspection should be useful for physical attributes and disposition, but certainly not at the same level as electronic inventory. Lastly, then would be the underpinning documentation, which might describe who ordered what and for what project or new hire, but could be many months removed.

Generating the Discovery Alignment Report

In the preceding sections, we discussed the classification of computer environment data sources and how to rank their usefulness by way of their primacy of evidence. This section is dedicated to showing you how to choose which discovery sources should be used in generating the Discovery Alignment Report, how to combine and present the findings in a Venn diagram, and then how to interpret the results.

The purpose of the Discovery Alignment Report is to measure agreement between all three discovery sources.

Thanks to René Descartes's categorical doubt, we know that our assets exist in the computing environment because they interact with each other, and modern computing environments are all about the interconnectivity of networks. There are switches, hubs, and bridges that create the physical and sometimes virtual pathways that make up the network. There are DHCP, DNS, and Active Directory services that control how and when individual computers and the network environment interact. And then, there are the separate services— e-mail, VoIP, file sharing, intranet sites—generating their own interaction logs and receipts to a surprising level of detail.

We also know from our discussion of the types of discovery data (EI, VI, and underpinning documents) that electronic inventory will give us the best data accurately and quickly. And we know from our discussion on the Primacy of Evidence, that we need to prioritize data sources that report as close to the assets as possible.

Pragmatic ITAM's stated goal is to build up trustworthiness of the hardware and software data so that the data you have about your IT assets is verifiably accurate and inarguable. If the reports coming out of the CMDB or Asset MDR are to be trusted, then the data coming in needs to also be trustworthy. *Pragmatic ITAM* requires that the discovered assets are confirmed by three distinct data sources before we can say with confidence these assets are part of the organization's computing environment.

The Rule of Three

Why three sources? As the song goes, three is a magic number[6]. In religion and mythology, the number three appears frequently. In cartography and navigation, your position is determined by measuring your distance against three points on a map (i.e., triangulation). In geometry and trigonometry, the triangle is the most basic two-dimensional form, and therefore, the most useful for axioms and proofs.[7]

For *Pragmatic ITAM*, three sources strike the right balance between useful and informative. More than three datasets become unwieldy to work with while fewer datasets mean the data patterns are undetectable.

So, which three sources do you use?

The first, and most important of the three is the discovery source from which the ITAM team is pulling software asset data. This data source will

---

[6] I would be remiss if I didn't point out the song "Three Is A Magic Number" is written in four/four time.

[7] The number three is also funny. True fans of Monty Python's Flying Circus can tell you all about the Book of Armaments, Chapter 2:9–21, from *Monty Python and the Holy Grail.*

be designated the Single Source of Truth (SSoT) for their subsequent reporting responsibilities, including:

- Software usage details
- The numerator for the software license compliance reports, and
- The basis for every volume license agreement negotiation and audit defense strategy

The software data source must have access to every relevant hardware asset in order to present a whole and complete picture of software usage within the corporate computing environment. This includes make, model, and serial number of the hardware, computer network name (like NetBIOS or the FQDN), and internal component details (video card details, CPU details, etc.) In short, almost all the critical fields necessary to create asset and configuration item records within the Asset MDR or the CMDB need to be available from the software data source.[8]

Most specialized SAM tools and ITSM platforms have their own discovery toolset to harvest these details. Other publishers have tools designed for a specific segment or platform. *Pragmatic ITAM* recommends using whatever tool a software publisher requires you to use when completing your yearly true-up reporting or responding to a license audit. That tool will almost always be mentioned in your volume license agreement documents (usually in the Terms & Conditions section).

For example, Microsoft's SCCM is the recommended tool for managing the Windows operating system, but it will only detect, report, and manage those systems. Given the ubiquitousness of Windows computers in the modern corporate environment, SCCM is an easy one to leverage. If there are other platforms in your ITAM scope, such as Apple computers or Linux/Unix servers, then other tools will be needed to discover them.[9]

---

[8] I mean something specific when I talk about "critical fields" and we will get to that in a later chapter.

[9] If you find yourself in a mixed computing environment, do not be afraid to leverage more than one SSoT; one for each family of assets. I recommend generating a separate Discovery Alignment Report for each SSoT, taking care to limit the other two comparative datasets to the SSoT's target. That way, you are confidently comparing Apples to Apples, and not Apples to Microsofts!

Choosing Scanning Tools to Assist in Discovery

The second discovery source should come from one of the networking control tools: DHCP, DNS, Active Directory, or the like. Dynamic Host Control Protocol (DHCP) servers usually do not keep enough information in their logs to be very useful. Domain Name Service (DNS) servers and Active Directory (AD) tools, on the other hand, can provide at least the computer's network name, the user's login name, and a timestamp of the login request. Plus, modern IT Security (ITSec) features within DNS and AD will prevent computers unknown to those systems from connecting with the network. In short, DNS and AD are great resources because, if those systems do not recognize a computer, then it categorically cannot be on the network.

The third source can come from anywhere, so long as it meets the following criteria:

• Penetrates the entire computing environment
• Contains at least one key field in order to compare and contrast with the other two discovery sources

There is one group within modern IT departments that maintains their own discovery scanning tools and can prove an invaluable relationship for your ITAM team: IT Security.

Leveraging IT Security Data

Of all the teams and groups within the IT department, IT Security (ITSec) usually has a scanning tool that meets the criteria of a third discovery source. Leveraging scanning data from IT Security also brings certain other benefits. Most IT Security departments have corporate policies and standards in place to permit them unrestrained access to scan the entirety of the computing environment. Further, best business practice standards require IT Security to maintain some sort of inventory for their own purposes.[10]

---

[10] In the case of IT Security, ISO/IEC 27000 provides standardization guidance.

IT Security typically has plenty of budget to invest in tooling and personnel to get their tools installed and running as quickly and effectively as possible. Most IT Security Managers are eager to demonstrate any return on investment from their efforts toward the greater good of the organization as a whole.[11]

Including ITSec in your discovery process can serve your ITAM team well in the long run. The relationship between ITAM and ITSec is continually evolving and the more direct value your ITAM team can show to ITSec, the better off both departments will be when the time comes to distribute the IT budget.

Key Fields: Computer Name Versus Serial Number

With our three discovery sources identified, our next step will be to reach out to the subject matter expert (SME) who can run a simple report of all the active computers within each source.

For this exercise, only basic information will be necessary, because, as mentioned earlier, the purpose of the Discovery Alignment Report is to measure *agreement* between all three discovery sources.

The first couple of iterations of this report will probably be manual, so too many details will be unnecessarily confusing and could introduce human error. Basic information need only be enough fields to help identify each individual asset within each dataset. At the bare minimum, the report should include the computer's network name, a date stamp of when it was last detected, the serial number, the user's login name, and the operating system name and version.[12]

When the SMEs deliver their reports, they will need to be compared and common entries flagged as a successful match. At least one key field will need to be designated to make the matches across the three separate

---

[11] There is a growing trend within IT Security to declare ITAM as a security concern. That discussion is outside the scope of this book, so *Pragmatic ITAM* will continue treating IT Security as a data customer.

[12] ITAM managers will not need all these details until Phase Three of the *Pragmatic ITAM* methodology, discussed later in this book.

dataset reports. When it comes to key fields, there are usually two to choose from:

1. The NetBIOS name of the device; or
2. The hardware's serial number

The NetBIOS name is the shortened form of the Fully-Qualified Domain Name (FQDN) registered with the DNS and AD services. The serial number is the manufacturer's identification number used to track the physical hardware through the manufacturing, selling, and support systems.

From ISO/IEC to ITIL to Asset MDR tool publishers, all will tell you it is not best business practice to use computer names for proper asset tracking. And they're right.

There are no hard and fast rules for computer naming conventions, so ITAM managers need to expect computer names to be changed at least a couple of times while an asset is in use. This is in contrast with the serial number that is physically stamped on the chassis, programmed into the onboard BIOS system of the computer, or available for lookup on the manufacturer's service support website. If the asset system is programmed to create an asset record for every computer name on the network, and the computer name changes, the MDR will then have two records for the same asset.

Unfortunately, not all network command and control tools or IT Security scanners harvest serial numbers for their purposes, but they should have NetBIOS and/or FQDN information. For the purposes of the Discovery Alignment Report, computer name will be sufficient, so long as the SSoT report possesses both computer name and serial number.

To put another way, the SSoT will behave as a Rosetta Stone of sorts, allowing the ITAM team to translate and associate computer names with serial numbers. This is exactly why, when detailing the requirements for an SSoT tool, *Pragmatic ITAM* explicitly mentions both NetBIOS and serial number. If an SSoT cannot deliver both, it is not much use as a single source of truth.

A note on virtual devices: virtual devices are a separate operating system environment (OSE) generated within a host computer or server with its own OSE. As such, it has no physical presence nor unique serial number. Different virtualization technologies have ways to differentiate individual OSEs from each other within the host or farm, and those could function as a serial number. ITAM teams need to use caution when choosing the right field to use as a *de facto* serial number for virtual systems. Select a field that does not or cannot be changed as the OSE moves through the asset lifecycle stages. Some examples include:

- VMWare uses UUID number
- Hyper-V uses BIOSserialnumber
- AWS uses EC2number

Generating the Venn Diagram

Once we receive the reports from network control, IT Security, and the SSoT, it's time to join all three together and report on where they agree and disagree. Venn diagram, like the one in Figure 3.1, are uniquely suited to present such information. Each dataset population is represented by a circle; where the circles overlap represents a data subset found in both (or more or all) dataset populations.[13]

Take, for example, Figure 3.2. The section labeled ABC is the count of data records found in all three circles. Sections AB, BC, and AC are data records only common to two data sources. And sections A, B, and C are unique to their data sets and not found on the other two reports.

Generating each section's numbers will take some doing. At the time of publication, there is no CMDB or Asset MDR that includes a premade

---

[13] "Three Rings for the Elven-kings under the sky,
Seven for the Dwarf-lords in their halls of stone,
Nine for Mortal Men, doomed to die,
One for the Dark Lord on his dark throne
In the Land of Mordor where the Shadows lie.
One Ring to rule them all, One Ring to find them,
One Ring to bring them all and in the darkness bind them.
In the Land of Mordor where the Shadows lie."
The Fellowship of the Ring, J.R.R. Tolkien (1954)

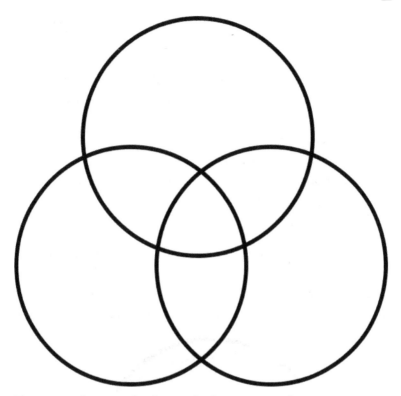

Figure 3.1 An example of a simple three-set venn diagram

report to generate a Discovery Alignment Report as a ready-made Venn diagram. More than likely, you will need some creative filtering to suss out the numbers for each population.

An alternative is a simple relational database. Upload the discovery source information into separate tables, then use the appropriate left and right join commands to derive the intended result. Still another alternative would be to use a spreadsheet and leverage a function command like "=MATCH( )" or "=COUNTIF( )" to calculate how many times particular computer names appear within each report.[14]

---

[14] Step-by-step instructions on exactly how to perform these activities are beyond the scope of this book. I recommend finding a tool master or SME who can devise exactly how to get your intended reporting tool to output the necessary answers.

When complete, Discovery Alignment Reports should present three different data outputs:

1. The individual record counts of each section of the Venn diagram
2. The percentage of each section compared to the sum total of all three discovery sources
3. A delta, or change, for either (or both) of the sections' record counts or percentage from one Discovery Alignment Report iteration to the next. Delta numbers can be very useful for identifying positive and/ or negative data trends and can make very effective Key Performance Indicators. We'll get into those a bit later on.

Wise counsel says to never deliver a report without double-checking your work. For Venn diagrams, the math is very simple. There is not much in the way of cross-checking delta calculations, but percentages will be accurate if every section added together equals 100 percent. The

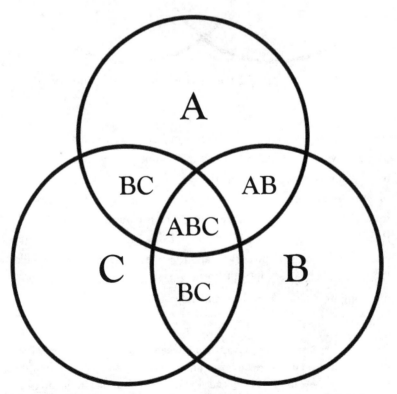

Figure 3.2 A three-set venn diagram with the shared sets labeled

population counts within any given circle should add up to the total number of records delivered by that discovery report. In our example diagram below, ABC + AB + AC + A equals the total number of records contributed by Source A. Test for each data source, just to be sure.[15]

- A + AB + AC + ABC = Source A total record count
- B + AB + BC + ABC = Source B total record count
- C + AC + BC + ABC = Source C total record count

Responding to the Discovery Alignment Report

The Discovery Alignment Report and its corresponding Venn diagram can't really be categorized as "right" or "wrong." After all, you only have the data and the data sources that you have available. However, upon completing an iteration of the report, there are both critical success factors and key performance indicators that will tell you whether your discovery is taking you in the direction you want to go.

Critical Success Factors

1. **All discovery sources scanning the corporate computing environment should agree.**
   This agreement is measured by the central section where all three datasets agree.

Key Performance Indicators

1. **Change rate of agreement continues to improve upward**
   This KPI seems obvious but it should be noted that 100 percent agreement will never happen. The point is the incremental improvement, measured in the change-rate (or delta) over time. So long as that number remains positive and continues trending positive over time, this KPI is in a good state. Should that not be the case,

---

[15] Funny thing about math: you would think everyone agrees about how to get an answer. My grandfather's favorite Abbott & Costello routine was the classic "7 times 13 equals 28" featured in their movie *In The Navy* (1941).

the ITAM team should look at the underpinning data to discover the source of the backslide.

2. **Change rate of AB, BC, and AC counts continues to improve downward, with explanations for outliers**

   Remember that these sections of the Discovery Alignment Report represent partial agreement, but not full agreement. If this KPI is not met, typically it will be because of a failure or omission of the third dataset.

   For instance, agents could be offline or disabled, meaning the computer was not available for an agentless scan.

   The task to improve these numbers falls to the SMEs responsible for the missing tool. How to transmit this work to the respective groups is up to the patterns of business of the individual IT departments. Incident or Problem tickets could be raised, thereby engaging those ITSM processes. Monthly status meetings between the ITAM team and the respective SMEs could serve as well.

   To really squeeze the most benefit out of this KPI, it's best to have written processes and procedures around how it is measured, and what happens next. (Most regulatory programs require this anyway). A written process will also resolve any questions about the veracity of this discovery data when a software audit occurs.

3. **Change rate of A, B, and C counts continues to improve downward, with explanations for outliers**

These sections represent unique entries by only one discovery tool. There are usually two explanations for these populations: either they are new systems entering the environment (and the other two discovery sources have not yet caught up) or they are old systems on the way out (and their entry in this discovery tool has not yet been removed).

The latter is easy enough to prove: the ITAM team should provide their asset lifecycle information to determine if all the conditions are met for removal. Of course, this assumes the ITAM team's data is at a point of maturity where it can provide proof positive of the asset's lifecycle state. How to get their data to that point is described later in this book. Until then, there is a real issue that this population will be in a holding pattern until the ITAM team can provide that data. But once that data is there, the SMEs of the discovery tools can confidently remove these entries with extreme prejudice.[16]

As to the former, there is the possibility that these are new entries. If so, then why were these devices added to the computing environment and not properly registered with the other discovery tools? It could be mere oversight or it could be something systemic. Depending upon what the ITAM team finds in their research, this population could represent a need for new enrollment processes to ensure these systems are picked up by the other discovery tools.

---

[16] *Apocalypse Now* (1979). Let's be clear: we are talking about deleting a data record from a **discovery source**, not the **managed data repository**. Deleting an MDR record risks irrecoverably losing other data attributes contained within that record which might be important later. But, any erroneously deleted discovery record would simply be recreated when the asset is discovered by the tool's next run.

CHAPTER 4

Starting Pragmatic ITAM: Phase Two

The ITAM Matrix Report

In the first phase of *Pragmatic ITAM*, we can prove we satisfied the ISO/IEC 19970-1:2017 requirements for their Tier 1 maturity model. This was done by the Discovery Tool Alignment report, with a heady dose of René Descartes's philosophical teachings as an anchor.

From this phase, we move up to Tier 2: Lifecycle Integration. The idea that information technology assets progress through the same standardized and measurable categories over and over again helps IT departments better align their activities with the rest of their business departments. The trouble is, most CMDBs and Asset MDRs (and even some ITAM managers) treat lifecycle flags as "nice to have." What should be an objective description of where the asset is in its useful life becomes subjective and loses its usefulness.

Pragmatic ITAM seeks to undo this lackadaisical treatment of the Asset Lifecycle and restore its subjective usefulness by way of the ITAM Matrix Report. But before we can talk about the report, we need to discuss what the Asset Lifecycle is.

By the end of this section, you will learn:

- What the Asset Lifecycle is and why it's so important to a functional ITAM program
- How *Pragmatic ITAM* defines an "asset"
- How you can use the Asset Lifecycle flags defined here to create an ITAM Matrix Report that will give you a simple way to visualize the state of all your assets at any given time

What Is an Asset?

Up to this point, we have not yet turned a critical eye to what we mean by an asset. The concept of Information Technology is generally agreeable, as is Management, so we will skip past those. But what is an asset? Definitions abound:

- Black's Legal Dictionary defines an asset as "the entire property of a person, association, corporation, or estate that is applicable or subject to the payments of his/her/its debts."
- ITILv3 Framework defines an asset as "Any Resource or Capability. Assets of a Service Provider include anything that could contribute to the delivery of a Service."
- Technopedia defines an asset as "a piece of software or hardware within an information technology environment."

These terms use different wording, but there are two commonalities: assets have a financial ownership component and a usage component. This two-pronged nature makes sense when we examine it within the larger concept of "information technology asset management." To manage these assets, we will need to know the asset's ownership and the asset's usage. We have already established a proof for usage: the asset must appear within the discovery system's record of note. Where will proof of ownership come from? From an organization's purchase records, maintained by the Procurement Team, value-added resellers (VARs), or publisher/manufacturers selling the assets.

This intellectual exercise has given us a precise definition of what an asset is, and a test to verify that an item is, in fact, an asset. Every CMDB or Asset MDR on the market has a field for Purchase Order or Invoice Record and a field for Discovery Date. If either of those fields do not have an entry in them, then we can assume that the required evidence hasn't been located. If either of those fields is complete, then we can assume (and verify) by going back to the record of note and confirming that, yes, this device or installation appears in this source. This, then, extends the ITAM team's mandate: to manage an asset, the source discovery record and source purchase record MUST BOTH be entered into the corresponding fields within the CMDB/Asset MDR.

The Asset Lifecycle

Before it's possible to dive in and create an ITAM Matrix, we must discuss the Asset Lifecycle, which looms large over the entire process. Simply put, all assets (regardless if they are hardware or software, virtual or physical) will go through the same steps over and over again. They are bought, made ready, deployed out to the field, recovered, and then either reused, recycled, or thrown away. Each and every CMDB and Asset MDR has a flag to report on an asset's lifecycle state. Some will use different terminology. Some will add or combine steps within the cycle. Some will allow the ITAM team to create their own flags. If there is any tool or process more critical to organized hardware and software asset management, this author has yet to come across it.

Figure 4.1 describes the asset lifecycle steps within the *Pragmatic ITAM* framework, along with similar terminology you may see in other ITAM methodologies or tools.

Steps	Definition	Also known as
Step One—Procured	Money, or the promise of money, has been paid for the possession of or right to use the asset.	Purchased, Acquired, Requested
Step Two—Inventoried	Asset has been physically received and is being made ready for use in the computing environment.	Delivered, Received, Processed, Making Ready
Step Three—Installed	Asset is active in the computing environment.	In Use, Deployed, Implemented, Active
Step Four—Recovered	Asset has been removed from the computing environment temporarily, with the intent it will be used again.	Returned, Fit for use, Recycled
Step Five—Disposed	Asset has been removed from the computing environment permanently and is no longer the property or concern of the organization.	Retired, Sold, Destroyed, Trashed, Removed from service, Donated

Figure 4.1 A simple 5-step lifecycle

Leveraging the Asset Lifecycle

Typically, the first questions business leadership asks of ITAM teams are around asset states:

- How many servers are in use?
- How many laptops do we have in the inventory?
- How many installations of a specific software are being used in a certain area?

An ITAM team with a good grip on their Asset Lifecycle flags will be able to answer those questions quickly enough.

And that is where the trouble begins.

Modern computing environments are dynamic by nature. Computers and servers are constantly brought into and out of the environment. Laptops get lost over the weekend. Software keys are shared with co-workers. Too often, these changes occur and ITAM teams are never notified to update the lifecycle flag.

This is the crux of the trustworthy data issue facing ITAM teams: how can a manually set flag ever accurately reflect the actual state of a dynamic reality? This problem should sound similar to the same questions René Descartes answers earlier in this book. Remember, Descartes proves his existence by recognizing he must exist for other items to interact with him. It doesn't matter if that interaction was really real, or a misinterpretation of his senses, or a dream, or some evil genius messing with his mind.

Just like Descartes, in order to prove something exists along the spectrum of the Asset Lifecycle, let's look to where that thing interacts with something else. To put it another way, let's change the definition of each of these five steps to set expectations for the kinds of data the ITAM team ought to receive. As an example, let's start with "Installed," because it is the easiest and the details were already discussed earlier in this book.[1]

Instead of defining Installed as "the item is being actively used in the computing environment," let's alter it to include an expectation. If something is being used, should it not be discoverable? And if not discoverable, then should it not appear in some other interaction? Say, for instance, a

---

[1] see: Discovery Source Alignment

trouble call into the Help Desk? Or a visual inventory, where an individual can log:

At [LOCATION] I saw the following serial numbers. Signed, [NAME] on [DATE]

If the asset suddenly stops appearing and can no longer be found, then it must not be considered Installed.

Consider the following chart, delineating each lifecycle step, definition, data expectation, and the potential sources that could provide that data:

State	Definition	Data Expectation	Data Sources
Procured	Money, or the promise of money, has been paid for the possession or right to use the asset	✓ Purchase Order or Invoice - Bill of Lading details - Visual Inspection - Electronic Inventory - Certificate of Disposal or Custody Change	Purchasing Department Value Added Reseller Manufacturer/ Publisher
Inventoried	Asset has been physically received, and is being made ready for use in the computing environment	✓ Purchase Order or Invoice ✓ Bill of Lading details ✓ Visual Inspection - Electronic Inventory - Certificate of Disposal or Custody Change	Receiving Department Inventory/Depot Manager
Installed	Asset is active in the computing environment	✓ Purchase Order or Invoice ✓ Bill of Lading details ✓ Visual Inspection ✓ Electronic Inventory - Certificate of Disposal or Custody Change	Electronic Inventory Service Management Asset Owner User
Recovered	Asset has been removed from the computing environment temporarily, with the intent it will be used again	✓ Purchase Order or Invoice ✓ Bill of Lading details ✓ Visual Inspection - Electronic Inventory - Certificate of Disposal or Custody Change	Receiving Department Inventory/Depot Manager
Disposed	Asset has been removed from the computing environment permanently and is no longer the property or concern of the organization	✓ Purchase Order or Invoice ✓ Bill of Lading details - Visual Inspection - Electronic Inventory ✓ Certificate of Disposal or Custody Change	Inventory/Depot Manager Disposal Company New owner of asset

Each corporation is organized differently, and these departments might not be named outright or may be named differently. But whatever person, group, or department is performing these necessary and critical business functions, they ought to be able to gather these data points and pass them along to the ITAM team.

Also consider that the data expectations of "Inventoried" and "Recovered" are the same. If an asset is brought out of service, and is deemed to still have some usable life left, it would need to be actively made ready for reuse, most likely by the same team that is making newly received assets ready for use. Some organizations might have a business need or desire to know how many reuses an asset undergoes before disposal. Those organizations will need to find some sort of differentiator data point to report on those events. Finally, and most important to *Pragmatic ITAM*, the number of Recovered assets is a direct indicator as to how well the ITAM team is reducing the cost-of-ownership of these assets. Every asset recovered and reused means a new asset does not need to be purchased!

Generating the ITAM Matrix Report

A list of assets and their associated lifecycle flags is helpful to an extent, but does not give us a full picture of the state of our computing environment. It is much more useful to have assets arranged in such a way that it's easy to see where attention needs to be focused for our ITAM data to be as complete as possible. For this, we have the ITAM Matrix Report, which will let us make snap decisions and prioritize and address any potential problems easily.

The ITAM Matrix Report will require a two-step approach. The first step is to organize the CMDB or Asset MDR records into a quadrant report, à la Pascal's Wager. We will use this report as a test or predictor to see if the asset record's Asset Lifecycle flag is set appropriately. The second step will then test and verify these flags are set correctly, and at the same time, fix the ones that are not.

Differences between hardware and software asset records will become important in this phase of *Pragmatic ITAM*. The ITAM Matrix Report will need to be repeated: once for hardware, and once for software (the reasoning will become clear in the next section).

The results of this exercise will be a verifiably accurate CMDB/Asset MDR that will:

- Provide a solid reporting foundation for software installation and license consumption reports
- Generate a handful of meaningful Critical Success Factors and Key Performance Indicators to track ITAM team's impact
- Provide reassurance to ITAM's data customers that their CMDB/Asset MDR reports are reliable and trustworthy

Step 1: The Four Quadrant Report

Thanks to the Discovery Source Alignment report, we have a verified and curated source of truth for the corporate computing environment. And thanks to our examination and definition exercise around the Asset Lifecycle steps, we know that anything on the Discovery Source Alignment report ought to be considered Installed within the environment. Lastly, thanks to that same exercise, we know that any asset flagged as Installed cannot be in any other state. The question "Is this asset Installed/In Use?" is now considered categorically bivalent, meaning the answer can only be yes or no.

Earlier in this chapter, we also reduced the concept of "ownership" into a bivalent question. If a specific asset has a purchase order (PO) and an invoice, then the organization has a fiduciary interest in that specific asset. That interest only ends with a properly recorded Certificate of Destruction. Without a PO/invoice, the ITAM team must continue their research to find the answer to whether the asset is owned and therefore relevant to their ITAM goals. No longer is the old idea of "possession is nine-tenths of the law" relevant. It is now ten-tenths.

We now have two tests that are both demonstrably bivalent and interrelated, which means we can leverage Pascal's Wager to help organize our data, discover knowledge gaps, and further validate the information coming out of the CMDB or Asset MDR. It would be optimal to generate this report within the CMDB or Asset MDR itself. At the time of publication, I am not aware of any CMDB or Asset MDR that has a report like this baked into the user interface. However, mostly all allow for a universal view or table view of all the hardware assets. The ITAM team

ITAM Matrix			
		Are we using it?	
		NO	YES
Do we own it?	YES	Quadrant #3: Inventory & Recovery	Quadrant #4: Optimal Implementation
	NO	Quadrant #1: Requires investigation	Quadrant #2: BYOD & Audit risk

Figure 4.2 A rendering of the four-quadrant ITAM Matrix report

can filter those views to obtain the numbers to complete the report. If your organization has not yet merged the purchase data with the electronic inventory data, it is still possible to complete this report manually in a simple spreadsheet or database.[2]

Step 2: Normalizing the Asset Lifecycle Flags

Another way to look at the first step of the ITAM Matrix Report is that it predicts how the Asset Lifecycle flag should be set. Consider Figure 4.2. Optimally, all the asset records that answer the "Are we using it?" question affirmatively, ought to have their asset lifecycle flag set to Installed, In Use, or something similar. At the same time, no Installed or in use asset flags should show up on the other two quadrants. That is what the second step intends to show.

---

[2] I would caution putting too much effort into building a database or spreadsheet to run the ITAM Matrix Report. In the time it takes to compare and contrast the EI data with the Purchasing data, the data itself will be almost too old to be relevant. Further, as you will see later in the book, such a manual report will have duplicated a healthy portion of the CMDB anyway. In the long run, it is best from a resource-investment perspective to regularly run this report only after both EI and Purchasing data is being regularly uploaded and/or inputted into the CMDB or Asset MDR.

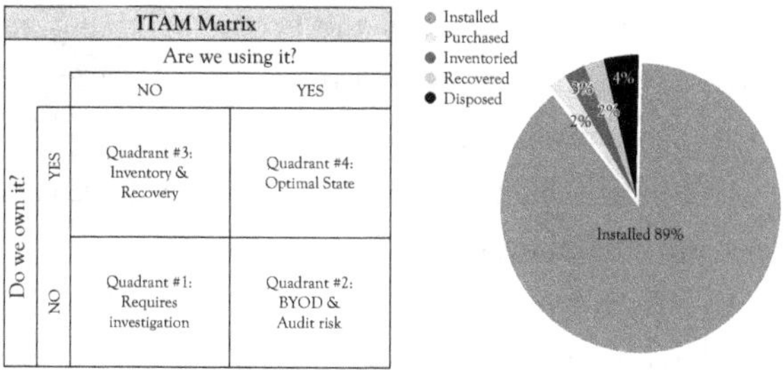

Figure 4.3 The four-quadrant ITAM matrix with quadrant 4 breakout (as a simple pie chart)

Pragmatic ITAM recommends a simple pie chart to break out the Asset Lifecycle flag for each quadrant. A typical report would look something like Figure 4.3.

At this point, the question arises, "Why make the distinction between owned and unowned assets?" The answer is that owned and unowned hardware are treated differently by software license agreements. Legal analysis is pretty clear (and aligns with the common sense notion) that you, as the hardware owner, are responsible for ensuring that the software installed on that hardware is duly-purchased.[3] But if you do not own it, what then? Hardware brought in by employees under a BYOD agreement is usually covered by user-based or "right of second use" use rights. But hardware that supports software or software as a service (SaaS) could be the responsibility of either the service provider or the customer. The answer, as any long-in-the-tooth SAM Manager will tell you, is in the contract. When in doubt, always go back to the beginning of the service agreement.

Using the ITAM Matrix on Software Assets: Fingerprinting

The obvious answer to the ITAM Matrix impact on software assets will be updating the hardware's lifecycle flags. As hardware assets move in and out of an Installed state, duly-purchased use licenses will need to be applied or recovered. This activity would have a direct impact on the corporation's

---

[3] "Due" in the legal sense, as something owed to a party, that is, "Due Process" is the legal process owed to the accused by the state. Therefore, "duly purchased" means that a purchasing process is followed (or, at least, has been) and completed for one party to properly pay another.

license position reports. But there is another story lurking in this data narrative that will become more useful to the overall trustworthiness of the CMDB/MDR: software fingerprinting.

Software modeling is taking individual software installation entries and aligning them into an umbrella license model. This is necessary because of a lack of consistency between how installed software is detected and displayed within the electronic inventory reports, and how the written license documentation describes the use rights granted to the purchaser. In the sample chart, a number of different installations can satisfy a number of different licensed use cases, all depending upon the wording of the license.

This many to many relationship (or n:n scenario) is difficult for computers to deal with. If there is no hard-and-fast rule that says "this means that" (a one to one relationship or 1:1 scenario) or "any of these things means this" (known as a many to one relationship or n:1 scenario) computers have a hard time knowing what to do.

Software Asset Management systems struggle with this activity: the attempt of taking the raw discoverable information and matching it to the software use rights the company actually has. Every SAM product on the market uses a slightly different strategy to figure out clear-cut relationships so their systems can correctly match the software installed to the use right you have duly purchased. This process is known as "fingerprinting."

Fingerprinting is not necessarily the same as normalization, although the end-product of both activities is a standardized and uniform nomenclature. Data normalization is a process where the different ways and meanings of data inputted into a field are made uniform. The following list is a normalization of a publisher's name, and all the ways it can be represented while still meaning the same publisher:

Publisher Name: displayed	Means	Publisher Name: normalized
IBM	}	IBM
IBM, Inc.	}	IBM
dba IBM	}	IBM
International Business Machines	}	IBM
1BM	}	IBM

The difference is that there is no association between different data sets. Regardless if the Publisher Name displays "IBM", "IBM, Inc.", or "International Business Machines," the meaning is the same: the name of the publisher of this product. With fingerprinting, we are inserting meaning (e.g., a relationship between two different data fields) that might not have existed before. Software installations described as "Funky Widget v1.2" and "Funky Widget v1.1" both consume the same duly-purchased use licenses called "Funky Widget v1." Nothing about the names of the installed software gives us any inkling of what licenses cover it.

Therefore, the ITAM Matrix is the perfect report to call out discovered software that has not (or cannot) be associated with duly-purchased use licenses. Figure 4.4 lays out the predictions nicely.

ITAM Matrix · Software		
	Are we using it?	
	NO	YES
YES	Quadrant #3: Newly purchased? Failed fingerprint	Quadrant #4: Optimal match
NO	Quadrant #1: XXXXX	Quadrant #2: Newly discovered? Failed fingerprint

(Row label: **Do we own it?**)

Figure 4.4 The four-quadrant ITAM Matrix report, focused on software assets only

Quadrant Four will contain all the properly associated installation and license records.

Quadrant Three will contain software licenses that have no matching software installations (either because the fingerprinting process has not been attempted, or there are no associated software installations to be matched).

Quadrant Two will similarly contain software installations that have no matching software licenses (either because the fingerprinting process has not been attempted, or there are no duly-purchased software license records to associate).

No records will qualify for **Quadrant One (i.e., No/No).**[4]

Responding to the ITAM Matrix Report

Critical Success Factors

1. **Every hardware asset in the organization's computing environment will have purchase and usage information recorded, in order to be considered a "managed asset"**
   Remember that purchase or usage information that cannot be harvested electronically will require manual effort to discover, rectify, and update the asset record. Organizations with immature discovery and procurement processes might take longer to get this information organized and presented to the ITAM team.

2. **Maximum number of assets are tracked in Y/Y quadrant**
   When an ITAM team begins following the tenets of *Pragmatic ITAM*, quadrant populations can be all over the place. But, as the team continues working through the methodology, more and more of the asset records will fall into Quadrant Four (Yes/Yes). Eventually, most of the asset records ought to be in Quadrant Four. If not, then something is wrong and the ITAM team should provide an explanation.

3. **Asset lifecycle flags are correct within +/- percent**
   This measure is about exception management and how well other teams—Service Management, Deployment, Inventory Management,

---

[4] Quadrant One represents CMDB/Asset MDR software records where there is no installation evidence (i.e., no mention in the Electronic Inventory SSoT) and no purchase records (that means neither the corporate Procurement team, the Value-Added Reseller, nor the Publisher themselves have a PO or Invoice). After twenty years in ITAM, I have never even seen a CMDB or SAM tool in such bad shape that such a software record exists.

and so on—are updating the CMDB/Asset MDR. If these teams are immediately updating the lifecycle flags as they receive, deploy, service, and retire assets, this measure will be very high. However, if the ITAM team has to constantly spend time fixing inaccurate asset lifecycle flags, it could signal underlying issues. Are staffing levels too low? Are standard operating procedures not being followed or do they need refreshing? Could more automation between management systems be a solution?

Key Performance Indicators

1. **The count of Unknown-Unknown Assets in Quadrant One continues to decrease, approaching 0 percent**
   This KPI is a direct measure of the ITAM team's effectiveness as they begin their work. All existing data is considered suspect until the ITAM team has been able to verify it. As procurement, disposal, and electronic inventory details are added to the CMDB or Asset MDR, this number will decrease. At the same time, the counts in the other three quadrants should increase to various degrees. Eventually, all the assets should be able to be moved out of this quadrant, either by electronic inventory, visual inspection, incorporating more SSoT inventories, or disposal activities. Any assets that cannot be moved out of this quadrant should have a ready explanation from the ITAM team.

2. **The count of Managed Assets continues to increase, approaching 100 percent**
   This KPI is a direct measure of the ITAM team's maturity. There will always be some outliers from the other two quadrants as the team discovers new purchases and deployments that slipped through the usual process controls. The real telling story in this KPI is the continual and incremental improvement. Any iterative variation in this number should have an explanation from the ITAM team (e.g., Merger & Acquisition activity).

3. **The count of Asset Lifecycle exceptions for each quadrant of the ITAM Matrix Report continues to decrease, approaching 0 percent**
   Inside the population of each quadrant, the Asset Lifecycle flag should be examined and any assets with a nonsequitur flag should

demand further inspection. For the "in use" quadrants, any asset record that is not flagged as Installed should be considered an exception and counted as part of this report. The same goes for the "not in use" quadrants, only the focus will be assets that are flagged as Installed. These asset records should have their Asset Lifecycle flag updated as soon as possible, as this will have a direct impact on software license and usage counts.

There will be exceptions to this KPI; some normal variants are listed in the following chart with potential tests to ensure these variants resolve themselves. Whether or not these variants need to be tracked as separate KPIs should be left up to the ITAM and IT leadership teams.

Situation	Lifecycle Flag	Notes
Systems being reimaged	Wrong flag: Installed Correct flag: Recovered (possibly Inventoried)	The modern trend is for "zero touch" or "factory imaged" hardware, where the new hardware will either be preconfigured for the corporate computing environment at the factory, or will receive those instructions upon first bootup by the end-user. However, reimaging of recovered systems (and subsequent destruction of critical data from the old user) should still be happening. To be reimaged, these systems might need to temporarily log into the corporate environment with an administrative account. They might also be online long enough to be discovered by an ITSec vulnerability scan or even the device's Command & Control system (read: SSoT). This might make the CMDB/Asset MDR *think* these systems are deployed when they are still with IT. The same AD login and IP Address segment should be enough to identify such devices, call them out as exceptions, and update the lifecycle flag.

Load balancers and offline recovery systems	Wrong flag: Inventoried Correct flag: Installed	Load balancers are tricky. They are supposed to sit there, all quiet, but at the ready, then bootup to handle a sudden surge in system demand: website activity, database record queries, and so on. While offline, our discovery tools might not pick them up. Also, our inclination is that, while offline, these systems should not consume any software license. However, there are software licenses where, even while offline, the device is required to be licensed. The best solution is to first confirm there is software on these systems that grants special licensing rights to load balancers and offline recovery systems. If so, tag these systems in the CMDB/Asset MDR with an appropriate "purpose" attribute,[5] and ensure your license consumption counts include these systems.
Project Go-Live or Mass Rollouts	Wrong flag: Inventoried Correct flag: Installed	Congratulations! The new site (be it branch, hospital wing, data center, or manufacturing complex) goes live next week! The work areas are ready to receive workers, with all their desktops and laptops and servers awaiting to be turned on and productive. Or maybe, as part of the initiation or kickoff celebration, the users will stop past a 'staging area' to pick up their equipment and set it up themselves. Either way—how does the ITAM program properly record these devices' asset lifecycle? If in the work areas, and powered on, but not logged into the network, are they really deployed? If they are resting in the staging area, awaiting pickup, are they really in inventory? These devices and their software should be flagged as Installed. As soon as they are pulled out of the generally available inventory population, they are serving a readily defined purpose— whatever project or rollout the project is focused on. The good news is, these exceptions will disappear as soon as the go-live or rollout completes. The devices will then behave normally (i.e., logging into the network, sending e-mails, updating records, etc.), which will then appear in the Discovery Tool Alignment report as expected.

---

[5] The next chapter will talk in greater detail about "purpose" data attributes, why they are important, and how to ensure that manual data is being properly collected and recorded.

CHAPTER 5

Starting Pragmatic ITAM: Phase Three

Database Integrity Quotient (DbIQ)

In Phase One, we verified that our Single Source of Truth (SSoT) is penetrating the entire computing environment. Phase Two helped ensure the Asset Lifecycle flags match with the usage patterns detected by the SSoT. In this chapter, we will ensure the data collected by the SSoT is sufficient for our ITAM needs, especially as far as software asset activities are concerned.

As stated before, most ITAM initiatives fail because they are overwhelmed by the sheer amount of data coming into the program. What we need is a way to organize the incoming data points to call out what pieces of information are missing and thereby direct the ITAM team's investigative resources to those critical needs.

René Descartes points us in the right direction with the concept of categorical doubt. We should not trust any data point (or, by extension, any data field) without knowing what it is telling us.

By the end of this section, you will learn:

- Why *Pragmatic ITAM* makes a distinction between asset records and configuration items
- A test for determining which data fields and points are germane to the ITAM efforts
- How to identify where that information can be found
- How to devise a strategy to track how well the ITAM team is doing in their research

Asset Record Versus Configuration Item

This is a good point to examine the similarities and differences between "asset records" and "configuration items," both of which play an important role in ensuring the accuracy and completeness of your CMDB, and consequently, your DbIQ.

Since the introduction of the concept back in the late 1980s, the difference between the two, the information each carries, and their respective purposes has never been made clear. Worse, CMDB and Asset MDR toolmakers will go their own way in organizing their databases and record sets, and may not even respect any differentiation at all.

For the purposes of *Pragmatic ITAM*, this section will attempt to make a clear delineation between the two concepts. In the end, we will see how their interplay will drive the future state of CMDB usefulness.

Key Definitions

According to ITIL, an asset is simply "any resource or capability." *Pragmatic ITAM* expands on this definition: an asset is any duly-purchased resource or capability intended to be used to further the organization's information technology goals.

Individual attributes of the asset will be entered into the asset record and all of the asset records will be rolled up into a specific managed data repository (MDR) called an asset register (in ITIL terms) or Asset MDR (in *Pragmatic ITAM* terms).

A configuration item (CI) in ITIL-speak is "any component or other service asset that needs to be managed in order to deliver an IT service." *Pragmatic ITAM* will not deviate far from this definition since it's workable for our purposes. Individual attributes of the CI will be entered into the configuration record, and all of the CI records will be rolled up into the configuration management database (CMDB).

On their face, these definitions do not provide any distinguishing details to determine one from the other. Swap the words "asset" for "configuration item" and you have the same thing. In fact, there are CMDBs in the market that actively avoid the distinction, and place all the asset and CI attributes into one record, and all those records into one table.

So why bother with the distinction at all? Because there is a distinction in the individual attributes carried within each record. And knowing the purpose of those attributes will make the distinction clear.

Purpose of the Asset Record

The attributes stored on an asset record should have three characteristics:

1. The attributes should be unique to the asset itself and found nowhere else in the CMDB/MDR system.
2. The information should be static and not expected to change drastically during the asset's lifespan.
3. The information should be delivered by a source with a high primacy of evidence.[1]

The concept of uniqueness is simply that these attributes do not appear in any other data table aside from the asset record. Attributes like serial numbers, make and model, CPU make and model, installed RAM, and video card should be expected to be found only in the asset record. If any other system or report requires these attributes, that system should be querying the asset records to retrieve, tally, sort, join, and so on.

These same asset attributes demonstrate a static nature. Laptops do not suddenly turn into server-class hardware. Serial numbers do not alter while in the field. Power supply ratings do not magically increase or decrease on their own. Network switches do not grow more ports while sitting in their racks overnight. Asset record attributes will trend toward set and forget; where the information is entered into the record fields once and will never be moved again. In fact, one could almost insist that the only attribute flag that will ever change during the asset's lifetime would be the asset lifecycle flag.[2]

---

[1] The concept of primacy of evidence—that data worthiness is dependent upon the proximity of the source to the subject—is discussed earlier in this book.

[2] Some assets do feature upgradeable components: CPUs, graphics cards, memory, onboard storage, et cetera. It is true that these components could be altered from the original buildout, and thus, require a normally static field to undergo a change. ITIL anticipates this, defining such attributes as *component CIs*. Whether or not a CMDB/MDR needs to track their *component CIs* to this level really depends upon how frequently such component upgrades occur and if the extra time and expense to track these components offers any benefit. But as information technology equipment becomes more commoditized and whole system swaps are the *de rigueur* solution for component failure, component change tracking becomes unneeded.

Purpose of the Configuration Item

CI attributes possess the mirror characteristics as their asset record relatives. CI attributes should be expected to change over time and not remain static: think purpose flags (development, production, backup), location and department details, IP addresses and DNS names, and assigned users. These attributes are not unique and are managed by other tables or services that make up the CMDB architecture itself (like Identity and Access Management services, Network Operations services, and Procurement systems). Categorically speaking, then, CIs should not be considered themselves to have a high primacy of evidence, but should point to systems (or other managed data repositories) that do.

In their defense, configuration items describe more than just assets. CIs are all the things and services that make up what the IT department delivers to the business. A good CI will focus on the relations, joins, and breadcrumbs that link the disparate system schema and retrieve key information necessary for the CMDB as a whole to report on the computing environment effectively.

Furthermore, CIs make it easier to build, report, and identify overarching issues, opportunities, and strategies on which the IT department can capitalize. Because of their relational database nature, they can easily encapsulate information from seemingly unrelated sources that wouldn't ordinarily exchange information and display it centrally.

CI attributes describe relationships between separate systems, so it should be expected that some asset record attributes would move over to CI attributes. *Pragmatic ITAM* prescribes that all the new and replatforming initiatives always start with IT asset management. In the beginning, there may be no other place to house attributes than on an asset record. As the CMDB system expands and matures—and communicates with more data repositories—what was unique, static, and low on the primacy of evidence scale should be replaced with CI references. For example, procurement information (PO and invoice numbers, dates, etc.) might start off as asset record attributes, but once the centralized procurement system begins communicating with the CMDB/Asset MDR, they should appear as CI attributes. The old data in the old asset records can be ignored in favor of the higher primacy of evidence coming directly from Procurement.

At the end of this exercise, everyone should be in agreement that the difference between an asset record and a configuration item is not that great. They should be considered two sides of the same coin: one containing the unique and static characteristics of a duly-purchased item used to create the computing environment, and the other joining and relating that information to other service delivery tools that make up the IT service management system.

The Two-Sided Coin Metaphor in Practice

Does this coin metaphor really add to the understanding of the CMDB/Asset MDR and the computing environment it should be modeling?

Let's examine a couple of scenarios real-life IT asset managers will face.

Hardware Assets

Hardware assets easily fit within our coin metaphor, and why shouldn't they? One can imagine our ancient Sumerian scribe would feel quite comfortable recording the physical attributes of a modern desktop computer on one side of his clay tablet, and all the systems that computer communicates with on the other.

But ownership has degrees, and many organizations will rent or lease computers, onsite servers, storage, and network security devices. Should ITAM teams track and manage leased and rented equipment?

Pragmatic ITAM says yes, for three reasons:

1. These devices are part of the physical makeup of the corporate computing environment, and changes made to them will have an effect on related CIs.
2. Lessees are legally obligated to treat the leased or rented equipment with the same duty of care as they would their own property.
3. At the end of the term, the leased or rented equipment will need to be replaced, and financial penalties will be incurred for equipment damaged, lost, or stolen. That financial impact will need to be tracked and tallied, and ITAM is the team with the tools and experience necessary to do so.

Software Assets

Software assets are trickier and could make our inner ancient Sumerian scribe panic. With software, is there something you can point to, with unique and static attributes and a high primacy of evidence for any other CIs attempting to reference it?

Yes. It's the use right.

A use right is the legal right to use, access, or implement another person's intellectual property for your own benefit. With that use right, there will be other attributes that will have no other place to be recorded than in an asset record. Characteristics like upgrade/downgrade rights, warranty end dates, localization rights, and so on., could be expected to be tracked on the asset record. For simplicity's sake, the transaction quantity of use rights in a single purchase could be recorded on one asset record, instead of individual asset records for each use right within the purchase. The CI for the software assets would contain the calculations necessary to compare the sum total of the use rights with the software installations (also CIs) that reference the physical location of the software in question.

It could be argued that a software asset record violates the "uniqueness" requirement and should really be a software configuration item in very large and mature CMDBs. Software asset records cannot calculate software license positions, as that would violate the "static" requirement for asset record attributes, so that information must be kept on a software CI. The use right quantity will be found within the Procurement system, and the ancillary use-right details will be recorded within the Contracts system. Information from those two systems ought to go to a software CI for all the license position calculations and generate the same results.

The *Pragmatic ITAM* answer is that the Procurement system does not describe actual things, but merely records the contractual transactions between buyer and seller. There still needs to be something to represent what has actually been passed between buyer and seller, even if it is a made up "straw man" representing a concept. ITAM's purpose is to track such "things," whereas Procurement does not.

Ask yourself, does Procurement have any concern where a chair is placed after it is delivered? Or a laptop? Or a server rack? Not usually. But ITAM does. And just as there are records for real-world items, then the same should go for ephemeral items like use rights.[3] Therefore, a software asset record is necessary.

Virtual and Service Assets

Virtual Assets are colloquially defined as virtualized desktop instances (VDIs) and operating system environments (OSEs) that exist within a shared pool of hardware resources. These shared resources can be a single physical server box (also called a "host"), or a cluster of such servers working together as a "farm."

Service Assets are VDIs and OSEs that exist on shared hardware provided by a cloud-based subscription service. Think Amazon Web Service (AWS), Microsoft's Azure, or Oracle Cloud.

Let us be clear about exactly why this scenario is different from the Hardware Assets and Software Assets examined previously. Obviously, the servers that provide the hardware resources should have their respective asset record describing their individual attributes. Also obvious is that the software use rights these servers will consume should have asset records as well. The question is the OSEs and VDIs themselves: should they have an asset record as well as their configuration item?

The *Pragmatic ITAM* answer is yes. Each discrete VDI and OSE will still possess unique and static attributes that will need to be recorded somewhere. These records can then be referenced by the hardware and

---

[3] Some could accuse me of using possibly spurious logic to accomplish an agenda. In my experience, using all sorts of Asset MDRs, the ones that support their license calculations with use-right asset records are more accurate and easier to understand than those that infer with CI links. In my defense, I offer up the same logical reasoning of the ancient Chinese cosmologists:

When asked what supports the turtle that supports the turtle that supports the four elephants who support the entire world on their backs, they responded, "It is turtles all the way down, and it is impolite to ask what lays beyond."

software CIs describing their interaction with the physical item or software use rights. Furthermore, treating both physical and virtual/ service assets the same will make asset reporting much easier and more consistent.[4]

Bring Your Own Device (BYOD)

In the early days of microcomputing (circa the 1970s and 80s), only businesses could afford cutting edge computing equipment. Few employees had personal computers of their own at home and the ones on the market were not what you would call portable. Even then, when given the chance, employees would usually buy a system that matched or mirrored the one sitting at their office desk. It was businesses that dictated what systems would be used and what software would be run with the end users having little to no say in the matter. As time and technology progressed, the target market shifted away from business to consumer and home electronics. The 2000s introduced laptops with the same power (and almost the same price point) as desktops, as well as Personal Digital Assistants (PDAs) like the Palm Pilot and Dell Axim, and eventually smartphones like the Apple iPhone. End users were now adopting the latest and greatest computing technology for their personal use much faster than corporate IT departments could keep up.

The concept of bring your own device (BYOD) was invented to keep the peace between tech-savvy end users and the corporate IT department. Users could use their own, personally purchased equipment on

---

[4] I will acquiesce on one point when it comes to Virtual and Service asset records. The ease at which these services can spin up and spin down VDIs and OSEs make them very attractive for development and proof-of-concept work. Granted, these servers tend to have notoriously short half-lives, and most publishers grant license exemptions to POC and DEV environments. I leave it up to the discretion of the individual asset manager if there should or should not be asset records.
Don't like that answer? "Turtles," I say.

corporate-provided networks and corporate-owned software. This created an interesting conundrum for IT asset managers: how do we effectively manage corporate-owned use rights and data on devices that are not owned by the business?

Most teams will not generate asset records for such devices, relying solely on the hardware CI that may be generated by an occasional discovery scan or secondary source. *Pragmatic ITAM* agrees, for no other reason than only corporate assets should be recorded within the Asset MDR. Furthermore, licensing rules and technology have caught up with this demand. Most BYOD licensing is now user-based, meaning the licensing travels with the user and the device they are immediately using, and data is not stored on a BYOD device, but merely displayed on the screen. Both feature trends make BYOD much less of a headache for IT Security teams as well. Should a user lose a device, licenses and data connections can be terminated from the corporate side.

Identifying Data Customers and Critical Fields

There are only two questions driving our activity in this phase:

1. Who is asking for ITAM information?
2. What ITAM information are they asking for?

Earlier in this book, we identified IT Security as one data customer. ITSec is keenly interested in how well their vulnerability scanning tools are penetrating the environment. ITAM is in the best position to report on that data since ITAM needs to know its SSoT is penetrating the same environment. IT Service Management (ITSM) is another data customer discussed earlier in this book, since ITSM requires verified user and Asset Lifecycle data to efficiently deliver their services. IT Finance (ITFin) is a third, as they will be interested in the relationship between consumed and unconsumed assets in their quest to maximize ROI and minimize TCO.

These departments are among the easiest to communicate and collaborate with because the discovery process often involves the ITAM team asking these very same departments questions and probing them for answers. By relaying back verifiably accurate data that helps them, a mutually beneficial relationship can flourish.

We need to examine what types of data customers we are dealing with because their needs will determine our critical fields.

ITSec, ITSM and ITFin are examples of *internal* data customers we need to consider.

Software publishers and the license auditors they employ are *external* data customers. Publishers and auditors are outside of your organization and their interests are separate from your organization's interests. Maybe parallel, like a good service provider should be, but let's not kid ourselves.[5]

Because publishers and auditors are outside of your organization, you cannot just call them up and ask them about their audit details to find out what data they need from you. (As any veteran ITAM expert will tell you, that will instantly trigger an audit!) The good news is, these data customers have already told you exactly what details they will expect from you should an audit occur (and one will eventually). Those details are buried within the master agreements (MAs), end-user license agreements (EULAs), volume license agreements (VLAs), and other underpinning documentation.

MAs, EULAs, and VLAs are legally binding contracts describing the relationship between the software publisher and the software user. Somewhere in them, the ITAM team will find language describing the nature of the use rights granted to your organization by the publisher. Two of the most common use licenses (see Figure 5.1 and Figure 5.2 for example text) are user-based licensing and computer-based licensing or device licensing.[6]

---

[5] Cerno Professional Services published a damning review of the relationships between the Big Four accounting firms and their software publisher clients. The results can be found in "Sleeping with the Enemy: How Major Audit Firms are Pursuing their own Clients" by Robin Fry (2018).

[6] A more detailed discussion of use rights, IP protections, enforcement schemes, and the like will occur later in this book.

User-Based License

Installation and Use Rights

Each user to whom Customer assigns a User SL must have a work or school account in order to use the software provided with the subscription. These users:

- may activate the software provided with the SL on up to five concurrent OSEs for local or remote use;

- may also install and use the software, with shared computer activation, on a shared device, a Network Server, or on ███████████████ or with a Qualified Multitenant Hosting Partner ("QMTH"). Rights to install and use the software with a QMTH do not apply if the QMTH is using a Listed Provider as a Data Center Provider, as those terms are defined in <u>Outsourcing Software Management</u>. A list of Qualified Multitenant Hosting Partners and additional deployment requirements are available at ████████████ This shared computer activation provision only applies to Customers licensed for ██████████ for business whens ████████████ for business is licensed as a component of ██████████████ ;

- must connect each device upon which user has installed the software to the Internet at least once every 30 days or the functionality of the software may be affected; and

- may use Internet-connected Online Services provided as part of ██████ [and governed by this OST]. Additionally, if permitted by Customer, users may elect to use connected services subject to terms of use other than this OST and with respect to which ██████ is a data controller, as identified in product documentation.
  - The Online Services will permit Customer to enable or disable these optional connected services; and
  - Customer is responsible for evaluating, enabling or disabling the availability to its users of optional connected services.

Figure 5.1 Sample text from a volume license agreement, describing user-based licensing

Device-Based License

Desktop Applications

Device License

1. Customer may install any number of copies of the software on a Licensed Device and on any Server dedicated to Customer's use for each License it acquires. Any dedicated Server that is under the management or control of an entity other than Customer or one of its Affiliates is subject to the Outsourcing Software Management clause.

2. Unless Customer licenses the software as an Enterprise Product or on a company-wide basis, it may also install the software on a single portable device for use by the Primary User of the Licensed Device.

3. Any number of users may use the software running on a Licensed Device, but only one user may access and use the software at a time.

4. Remote use of the software running on a Licensed Device is permitted for the Primary User from any device or for any other user from another Licensed Device.

5. Remote use of the software running on a Server dedicated to Customer's use is permitted for any user from a Licensed Device.

Figure 5.2 Sample text from a volume license agreement, describing device-based licensing

For these two examples, what kinds of critical data do we need to collect? For the user licenses, the auditor will ask for the **user names** (1st critical field) on each **computer** (2nd critical field) where their company's (3rd critical field, **publisher name**) software (4th critical field, **software name**) is installed.

For the device licenses, the list is nearly the same apart from the absence of any mention of who is using the computer. In the case of device licenses, the publisher is only concerned about the count of computers with the software installed.

This overlap of requirements is not accidental, and can be used to the ITAM team's advantage. Software publishers and auditors have no quarrels with sharing information, strategies, and techniques between themselves. Publishers will stick to the same scheme throughout their product's sellable life. Also, smaller publishers will usually adopt whatever licensing scheme the larger firms use (think Microsoft, Adobe, Oracle, IBM, etc.). So much so that experienced ITAM professionals can almost recite the most popular data fields necessary for responding to audit requests from memory.[7]

Calculating the Database Integrity Quotient (DbIQ)

We now have a list of the data points necessary for ITAM to be successful, to both internal and external customers. Some of that data is coming into the CMDB/Asset MDR automatically (as is the case with the SSoT) and some will be entered in by hand (as is probably the case with the software license details). What is needed now is a measure that will track how many of these data points are not yet known, and how much progress the ITAM team is making in learning them. For that, we turn to the Database Integrity Quotient (DbIQ).

"Database Integrity," for the purposes of *Pragmatic ITAM*, simply implies we are looking at how complete a database's dataset is. A quotient is merely a ratio between two numbers: a numerator and a denominator. For our purposes, the denominator will be the total number of critical

---

[7] The chart in Appendix A, Common Critical Fields, lists the usual suspects with a short reasoning as to where the data fields become necessary.

$$IQ = \frac{n_1 + n_2 + n_3 + \cdots + n_f}{t * f}$$

t - total number of Managed Assets records

f - total number of critical fields contained on each record

n - number of records which contain data within that critical field

Figure 5.3 Simple formula for creating a quotient

fields within our database, based on what our specific data customers need. The numerator will be the count of asset or CI records containing data in those fields. Figure 5.3 lays it out as simple formula. This quotient can be multiplied by 100 and expressed as a percentage.

The percentage of completeness can be measured at regular intervals to give a visual representation of the ITAM team's progress over time. Plotting these intervals should produce a trend line graph pointing up, like in Figure 5.4.

Every CMDB/Asset MDR records its critical asset information differently. In order for the DbIQ to have meaning, ITAM teams and their leadership need to have a clear understanding of how their CMDB/Asset MDR places information into its tables. For example, purchase order and invoice information are required fields. Some solution providers treat these fields as part of the asset record itself while others keep the information in another table for their procurement services, then relate the

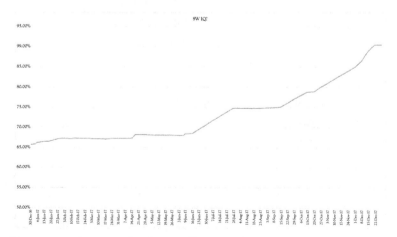

Figure 5.4 An example of a trendline graphic, showing steady improvement of the DbIQ over time

information back to the asset record. That situation sets the possibility of the procurement table and the asset table not having the same values for the DbIQ calculation, resulting in confusing and divergent DbIQ metrics. While your team may not be able to change how your specific solution provider handles this kind of information, you can make sure they are aware of how it works in regards to this kind of information and can easily troubleshoot if there is a discrepancy.

Responding to the Database Integrity Quotient (DbIQ)

The ideal is for the DbIQ to reach 100 percent, where every asset record within the CMDB/MDR has every critical field filled in. Like all ideals, we should expect the DbIQ to fall short.[8] The usefulness of the DbIQ, then, is in the trending; how close can we get to that ideal 100 percent over time?

For IT leadership, so long as the DbIQ continues to trend toward 100 percent, that demonstrates that more data is being added to the CMDB and therefore, you are getting more trustworthy dashboard outputs. Any deviation from that trend should have an explanation associated with it. Potential causes of a deviation could be any number of things: business acquisition and divestiture activities, large procurements not following the prescribed workflow, data connections between the source and the CMDB/MDR going down, and so on.

For the ITAM team, the DbIQ will point them to where knowledge gaps exist. The ITAM team should be examining which critical fields are usually missing on the asset records and either:

1. spend the time to enter that information manually or
2. invest the resources to have that information automatically populated from the trusted source.

---

[8] NPR's *Prairie Home Companion* would sign off their "News from Lake Wobegon" skit with a friendly "Well, that's the news from Lake Wobegon, where all the women are strong, all the men are good-looking, and all the children are above average."

Do not discount the value of asking vendors or value-added resellers (VARs) to add more information to their advanced shipping notices, or software distributors to ensure software title, stock-keeping unit (SKU) and volume license contract number are included in their license management portal.

Although this very chapter warned you against asking publishers for details on their licensing agreements and other data requirements mere paragraphs ago, these requests can be couched in such a way as they will not trigger an audit. In this case, you're not asking what they need from you (e.g., what data will be requested in an audit), you are asking that they provide you with more data for your own record keeping.

Critical Success Factors

1. **How close is the DbIQ to 100 percent?**

   You should not expect your DbIQ to ever reach 100 percent. Rather, we want to track the trend of the DbIQ with each iteration and verify that it is moving toward 100 percent.

   Furthermore, at some point, the DbIQ improvements will shift away from direct data entry by the ITAM team (i.e., manually inputting data) to indirect, automated feeds (i.e., no human inputs needed). When this shift occurs, this CSF will become less informative, but the exception reporting (see following related KPI) becomes even more critical.

2. **What is driving any drastic changes in the DbIQ? (i.e., changes to the critical field list, changes in the computing environment, issues with underpinning sources)**

   Should the DBIQ suddenly trend down (e.g., away from 100 percent), especially in a significant way, the ITAM team ought to have an explanation. If there is no readily discoverable explanation, there are deeper issues with your ITAM process that must be addressed and tracked through resolution.

   Furthermore, as the overall trend plateaus close to 100 percent, the ITAM team will list out more exceptions and issues preventing continual improvement. Not only does this indicate maturity of the

ITAM program, but it will begin to identify where the next round of automation efforts will have the most impact.

Key Performance Indicators

1. How many critical fields are identified?

There is not a correct number of critical fields that will be applicable for every organization. Rather, the right number for your ITAM team is the right number for your data customers.

This number forms the denominator, or the bottom half, of the quotient. Any changes in this number need to be called out, along with the reasoning behind the change, because any increase or decrease in this number means something has changed in what data attributes the ITAM team needs to collect.

2. Which critical fields are missing information, or lagging behind others?

If a field is usually populated automatically with data from another discovery source, the sudden disappearance of that data signals a problem with that automation.

If a field is hand-entered after research by the ITAM team, lagging data entry could be a sign of trouble beneath the surface. The team could be getting pulled away from this project to concentrate on another matter (responding to an audit, assisting with a new merger & acquisition, etc.) It could also mean the ITAM team is having trouble accessing the underpinning documents containing the data they seek. In either case, leadership should be prepared to step in and remove whatever roadblocks are preventing these data attributes from getting into the CMDB/Asset MDR.

3. How many exceptions exist that prevent data from reaching these critical fields?

At the beginning of the DbIQ reporting, there will be a long list of explanations and challenges (possibly even a few excuses) as to why data is missing. It stands to reason that as the ITAM team works through them, the number of explanations and challenges preventing them from completely filling out all the required data attributes should trend downward. Anything new suddenly challenging them or throwing them off their upward trajectory should be a signal for concern by leadership and maybe a need for their intervention to clear the underlying issue.

Starting Pragmatic ITAM: Review

You have made it halfway through the book. By now you should have a firm grasp on the basics of the *Pragmatic ITAM* methodology and should be starting to put together your own ideas as to how the effective application of this methodology will have a positive impact on your business goals.

There has been a lot to digest in the previous three chapters, so we are going to take a moment here to review the most salient points we covered and tie them back to the central tenets of *Pragmatic ITAM* as well as the core philosophical underpinnings we first explored at the beginning of the book.

Let's start by reviewing the central tenets of *Pragmatic ITAM*, which are:

1. Knowledge of the problem inherently changes the nature of the problem
2. She with the best documentation wins
3. Work smarter, not harder
4. Trust, but verify
5. Asset lifecycle management requires rigor
6. Process is a means to an end, and is not an end itself

These tenets form the basis of the *Pragmatic ITAM* methodology and as you start to internalize them, they should aid you in developing (or improving) your own ITAM program over time.

Phase One and the Discovery Tool Alignment (DTA) Report

In the first part of this chapter, we discussed how to create your Discovery Tool Alignment report, which will help you to understand which data sources you need to use in tandem in order to get a complete picture of your computing environment.

In the ISO/IEC 19770-1:2017 guidelines, Tier One maturity of an ITAM program requires "trustworthy data," which is one way to describe this data picture you're creating.

We can easily tie this back to Descartes, who posited that *things exist because they interact with other things*. The DTA report graphically presents where your discovery and management tools agree and disagree, based on how your existing assets are interacting with one another and with your discovery tools. It identifies exactly which devices the ITAM manager (or team) needs to focus their inventory and research activities on and also predicts what kind of result further ITAM inventory activity and research will find.

How does this process relate back to the central tenets of *Pragmatic ITAM*?

1. Knowledge of the problem inherently changes the nature of the problem
   Once you know which of your discovery sources are most useful as well as where you have shortfalls, you can focus your attention and energy much more efficiently.
2. Trust but verify
   Each discovery source bills itself as reliable, but only by using multiple sources and finding alignment can you really trust the data you receive.

Phase Two and the ITAM Matrix Report

In the second part of this chapter, we introduced the ITAM Matrix Report, another essential way to organize and display your ITAM data.

ISO/IEC 19770-1:2017 guidelines indicated that Tier Two maturity of an ITAM program requires "lifecycle integration" for your IT assets, allowing the business to achieve greater efficiency and cost-effectiveness. Lifecycle integration means being able to accurately apply lifecycle tags to your assets so you know, for certain, what state they are in and with which assets you need to be concerned.

Earlier, we learned from Pascal how to leverage data to drive decision making. The ITAM Matrix Report allows us to take our lifecycle data and turn it into an easily readable status report of all our existing assets, then use that data to make informed decisions.

The ITAM Matrix Report also:

- Provides the basis for automating asset lifecycle assignation and improving CMDB/Asset MDR accuracy

- Highlights unexpected changes in the computing environment so the ITAM manager (or team) can address
- Over time, lends transparency as to the measurable impact of the *Pragmatic ITAM* methodology

In this section of the book, we can see fully represented these tenets of *Pragmatic ITAM:*

1. Asset lifecycle management requires rigor
   This one is fairly self-explanatory. Creating the ITAM Matrix Report means assigning lifecycle flags to your assets. To engage in this process successfully requires rigorous attention to detail.
2. Process is a means to an end, not an end itself
   The process of creating the ITAM Matrix Report ends with a fully realized record of your existing assets. Getting to this end report in a specifically directed way is not required for maximum usefulness of said report.

Phase Three and the Database Integrity Quotient (DbIQ) Report

In the final part of this chapter, we covered the Database Integrity Quotient (DbIQ) Report and how this level of data collection opens up opportunities for further ITAM program optimization, resulting in potential cost savings as well as important available data in the case of a software license audit.

Indeed, the ISO/IEC 19770-1:2017 guidelines for Tier Three ITAM maturity expects "optimization" by leveraging the results from the previous tiers to drive more efficient and effective asset management processes.

We can easily relate this back to our friend Socrates, who taught us to expect our understanding of a given situation to improve over time, as we gain access to more information. The DbIQ report can be used as an indicator of how effective the ITAM manager (or team) is in locating the necessary data attributes to:

- Accurately measure software license usage and consumption
- Correctly answer reporting requests from data customers (including software license auditors)

- Identify license audit risks and reallocation opportunities to avoid un-budgeted penalties and reduce budgeted expenditures

The tenets represented in this phase of the *Pragmatic ITAM* process are:

1. Work smarter, not harder
   The DbIQ can help drastically narrow the focus of the ITAM team. The DbIQ can also work as an early warning system because if it starts to trend toward less reliability, they will know immediately if something is wrong without having to constantly review all the available data.
2. She with the best documentation wins
   Your DbIQ is proof positive that the data you have collected is inarguably accurate. It is this proof that will be the nail in the coffin of the next auditor that comes looking for errors.

What All This Means

We can expect to see a few key results from going through this three-phase process:

1. The CMDB's data becomes more accurate, reliable, and trustworthy, which will promote further automation and adoption.
2. The CMDB/Asset MDR reporting becomes the source for data-supporting business decisions, including accurate budgeting, consumption, purchasing and audit defense.
3. The CEO, CIO or CFO who owns the *Pragmatic ITAM* process is venerated as a rock star![9]

---

[9] The counterpoint is Molly Shannon's *Saturday Night Live* character, Mary Katherine Ghallagher, and her "Superstar!" catchphrase.

Looking Ahead

In the second half of this book, you can expect to find:

- Recommendations for maintaining the new precision and usefulness of the CMDB/Asset MDR
- Guidelines for how to craft relevant corporate policies, standards, and processes
- How to locate, hire, and train the right employees to become successful ITAM managers and team members.
- Predictions on how ITAM will evolve in the future and eventually end.

CHAPTER 6

Weaponizing Your ITAM During Mergers, Acquisitions, and Software License Audits

This book has shown you the critical elements of building a successful ITAM program. The *Pragmatic ITAM* methodology is designed to help you, as a technology leader, and your ITAM team to develop a cache of data that's irrefutable and inarguable.

It's time to consider who is going to come along eventually and try to refute and argue with what you know to be true. Maintaining a successful ITAM program means being ready to leverage your data in the adversarial scenarios that are likely to arise.

ITAM in Action: Mergers, Acquisitions, and Divestitures

As you go through this chapter, you'll start to see a pattern: your verifiably accurate ITAM data will be most valuable at times of upheaval. It's not a coincidence that software audits often coincide with major organizational changes—but *Pragmatic ITAM* aims to ensure that your data is at the ready, no matter what else is going on in the company.

A merger, acquisition, or divestiture (M&A)[1] is nothing if not a time of upheaval and minor organizational chaos.

---

[1] For the purposes of clarity, we'll use "M&A" to refer to mergers, acquisitions and divestitures. Each is a unique scenario, but in ITAM terms, it will present similar challenges.

M&As don't happen very often, which makes them kind of exciting, like when you had a pizza party in school. It's not really about the pizza, it was more that you got to do *something different* for a day.

The excitement factor is one reason that when an M&A presents itself, everyone wants to be involved. These situations are typically very visible to business leadership, thrusting teams that don't normally get their due into the spotlight, which can be a great thing if you have a team that's doing great things.

Your ITAM team can certainly be one of those departments that suddenly finds itself the center of attention, but it's usually not exactly exciting for them. Indeed, these situations can be quite dangerous from an ITAM perspective:

They're Distracting

Because M&As don't happen that often, a lot of past mistakes get repeated. Even if a process was once put into place to deal with M&As, chances are the last one was so long ago that no one is even around to dig up the documentation. It's also more than likely that no one at the organization has ever gone through one before, meaning a lot of opportunity for errors.

They're Highly Visible

It's true that people get excited about the potential visibility of this type of project, but when leadership is paying close attention, things can get stressful. In an M&A scenario, your corporate leaders have a lot at stake and a low tolerance for failure including cost overruns, completion delays, or scope creep. That adds up to tremendous pressure for an ITAM team that may not be used to working under such scrutiny.

They're an Audit Risk

Software publishers and auditors will watch for M&A announcements and wait until the company is fully distracted to spring an audit. The distraction makes your organization vulnerable—the fewer resources you have to devote to the audit process, the more likely you are to make concessions. In addition, license agreement terms and conditions around corporation to corporation activity are usually buried in contractual language and easily overlooked, presenting another opportunity for simple mistakes to slip through the cracks.

Preventing ITAM Issues During Mergers, Acquisitions, and Divestitures

M&A scenarios can happen on virtually any timeline. You may have a lot of time to prepare or not much at all. Once you find out that your organization will be facing an M&A, the ITAM team should start preparing as soon as possible.

1. Get the ITAM team involved early in the process

IT Security

For mergers and acquisitions, ITSec will want to assess security and vulnerability issues within the acquired company. *Pragmatic ITAM* will help ensure ITSec tools are penetrating the environment correctly and completely with discovery source alignment.

For divestitures, ITSec will want to know exactly when all divested assets are gone in order to free up their own resources. *Pragmatic ITAM* will help ITSec speed up that process and ensure accuracy because the ITAM team will have at-a-glance visibility into asset lifecycles in the ITAM matrix.

IT Finance

Nothing throws off the cost/benefit analysis for an M&A like an unknown cost or penalty lurking within the acquired company. *Pragmatic ITAM* is designed to unearth "gotchas," so there are no surprises.

Most M&A activities are measured by how quickly and completely expected monetary gains are realized. The sooner ITFin learns the overall financials of the incoming or outgoing company, the sooner it can report success. *Pragmatic ITAM* is designed to get that information into a trustworthy state quicker than ITFin can do alone.

Project Management

A good Project Manager (PM) will want help at the beginning of the M&A by identifying knowledge holders, setting scope and boundaries for the M&A project, and ensuring expectations are met. The ITAM team will possess a great deal of this information already, thanks to the *Pragmatic ITAM* method.

2. Get comfortable with running two ITAM teams for a while

In an M&A, the asset records and CIs for each company will need to be kept separate until the service and license agreements are renegotiated to account for the combined group.

In a Divestiture, the question is about time—the less prepared the receiving organization is (if they are prepared at all), the more pressure will be on the original ITAM team to track the outgoing assets for them, until they are ready.

3. Get control of what existing software publishers and service providers know about the M&A plans

Software auditors routinely scan trade papers for public reporting and press releases and use the information to schedule audits at times that are inopportune for you. This means you and your ITAM team should be ready for an audit notification as soon as anything about your M&A or divestiture goes public.

Software publishers and service providers know a great deal about your environment, and the environment of the M&A target, based on the purchasing activity and service support requests. Do not assume that they'll be coming into an audit with little information— they may well have more than you if you are dealing with an organization that has a less robust ITAM process in place.

Ensure communications between both companies and the software publishers/service providers are limited to a "need to know" basis, so they do not know more about the M&A deal than is required.

4. Expect audits and address immediately

In the confusion of the M&A, responsibilities get shifted, knowledge holders leave, and official communications can be lost. Software publishers and auditors are counting on it. A good Project Manager (PM) should be on the lookout and expect to act as a central point of contact for any official letters, e-mails, or declarations of intent to audit.

If and when an audit is declared, immediately activate your Audit Response Process.[2]

5. Do not be afraid to bring in outside experts to help

Software publishers will routinely bring in a third-party software auditor to help them conduct their investigation... so why don't you? It is well within your right to have knowledgeable counsel when facing a software audit that could mean millions of dollars of unbudgeted expenses.

There are a number of third-party service providers that can help guide you through an M&A situation. Some specialize in IT aspects of M&A while others focus on specific software publishers. Your CMDB or SAM tool provider might be of assistance, especially if there are technical features of their tool that could be useful in the M&A project.

You should be able to find an expert that can help you address your specific concerns or who can point you to someone who can.[3]

Software License Audits

Software license audits are the single biggest event for ITAM professionals. In many ways, these audits are their raison d'être. Whether they happen in the context of an M&A or at another time in your organization's history, being prepared for them should be your ITAM team's number one goal.

The Auditor

Software license audits are conducted by—you guessed it—software license auditors. These auditors may be specifically employed by the software publisher conducting the audit or they may be third-party "independent" auditors hired by the publisher for the purpose of your specific audit.

---

[2] What do you mean you don't have one? Don't worry, just keep reading.

[3] My company, Boerger Consulting, LLC, is just one outside ITAM consultant that can help you prepare for and weather an audit.

Auditors are the ultimate data customer. Your ITAM team's goal should be to provide them with all the data they need and have requested as efficiently as possible. Note, the goal is not to provide them with all the data you have.[4]

In the audit process, you are, in effect, doing battle with the auditor. That doesn't mean you should treat an auditor as your enemy, but you should always be aware of their possible intentions.

You have an advantage in the audit process in that you already know exactly what information the auditor will use against you. It's all laid out in black and white in your software licenses, agreements, and Terms and Conditions. Your audit response should include going through this documentation and making sure that you have data that directly aligns with those agreements.

The Audit Response Playbook

No matter how prepared an ITAM team is, without support from the business leadership itself, they cannot perform at their peak ability and successfully navigate an audit. An audit response playbook should give corporate leadership and ITAM teams a framework for addressing a software audit as a united front and achieving the best possible outcomes for the business.

Every ITAM team should develop their own specific Audit Response Playbook.

A successful audit playbook should act as a reference for every member of the ITAM team to standardize the software license audit process from an internal perspective.

---

[4] Crash Davis: "...You having fun yet?"
Nuke Laloosh: "Oh yeah, I'm having a blast. Thanks."
Crash: "Good."
Nuke: "Sucker teed off on that like he knew I was gonna throw a fastball."
Crash: "He did know."
Nuke: "How?"
Crash: "I told him."
Bull Durham (1988)

The two most important steps for creating a successful audit playbook are:

1. Creating specific policies, standards, and procedures to enforce the overall software license strategy.
2. Writing it all down so everyone knows what to expect during the audit process (this is the "playbook" piece of the puzzle).

Next, I will outline how the software audit process works and what should be included in your playbook to successfully address each stage of the audit.

The Five-Step Audit Process

1. Declaration

What Happens: Somehow, some way, the software publisher has to inform you that they are exercising their right to audit your software licenses.

How to Address in Your Playbook: What the notification looks like, who is to be contacted, and how long you have to respond should be detailed in the software license agreement itself (either in the contract boilerplate, the Terms and Conditions addendums, or the use license documentation). Your playbook should include an explicit accounting of who (whether it's a team or an individual) an audit notification must go to in order to be considered valid.

In normal times, this information is used to program the SAM tool's software license position reports. In an audit, someone from ITAM should be going through these sections with a fine-toothed comb, making sure your information is as accurate as possible.

2. Fact Finding

What Happens: You and the software publisher (and sometimes the "independent" auditor) meet to define the scope of the audit: what needs to be reported, what reporting scripts or programs are to be run on which systems, what details about which accounts are being requested, and so on.

How to Address in Your Playbook: You'll want to be able to refer to your audit response playbook during fact finding for the standards your auditor and software publisher need to meet. Specifically, you'll want to outline how the auditor and/or publisher are expected to protect customer and client PII, PCI, PHI, or other privileged information. Your playbook guidelines should include how this data is transmitted from you to them, how they access the data (programs, required encryption, etc.) and how the data is otherwise secured when in their possession.

During this stage, you'll also want to use your playbook to establish which internal teams have which RACI designations, including determining the Single Point of Contact (SPOC) who will be working directly with the auditor and software publisher and determining the Subject Matter Experts (SMEs) for the tools to be used for gathering the required installation data.[5] In addition, you will want to make sure your playbook specifically addresses who exactly (in order to set timeline expectations) needs to approve or sign-off on purchases, contract changes, new license agreements, and so on.

3. Reporting

What Happens: The auditor will take all the data gathered from the reports, scripts, and installation details from your computing environment back to their location to compare against your purchasing receipts and invoices to determine shortfalls and (rarely) overages.

How to Address in Your Playbook: It's all in the auditor's hands now. Nothing for ITAM to do but wait.[6]

However, it should be noted that after the auditor comes back with his findings, ITAM does not have to merely accept what they found as fact. Audit reports can be full of errors and assumptions, so a good ITAM manager will not take the auditor at his word. When the report comes back, the ITAM team needs to go through it as carefully as they did their own data when they were in fact-finding mode.

---

[5] We'll talk a bit more about RACI designations in the next chapter, but know it stands for Responsible, Accountable, Consulted, and Informed

[6] "The waiting is the hardest part."—Tom Petty

4. Negotiation

What Happens: The final report will be presented to all the parties, with a price tag attached. What that final price tag will be depends upon all the factors taken into consideration during the audit, and at this juncture, should not come as a huge surprise.

How to Address in your Playbook: Your playbook should indicate any contract additions, addendums, and exhibits the corporation will require to be present for any new software license agreements coming out of the audit to be considered "valid." During negotiation, these requirements must be met before any agreements can be reached.

5. Resolution

What Happens: Once all the parties are in agreement on the cost, documents can be signed, monies handed over, and everyone goes back to business as usual.

How to Address in Your Playbook: Your playbook should outline how any penalties are to be divided between department cost centers or internal customers (or if the IT budget bears the brunt).

Recommended Do's and Don'ts for Successful Audit Responses

DO have an Audit Playbook with supporting Policies, Standards, and Procedures ready before you receive an audit notification	DO NOT expect any auditor to abide by Policies, Standards, and Procedures dated after the fact
DO keep your SPOC and final audit approver as separate roles for "good cop/bad cop" negotiation tactics	DO NOT have the same person play the role of SPOC and who will sign off on the final resolution
DO carefully examine the final report for errors, duplicated entries, and bad assumptions	DO NOT assume the software publisher or the auditor know your internal systems better than you
DO request a copy of their records and compare to your own during the fact-finding phase (as is your right)	DO NOT assume your organization's purchasing records match the software publisher's receipts and invoices
DO work to keep the scope of the fact-finding phase limited to only the software titles and installations germane to the audit itself	DO NOT assume that the auditor will not "tattletale" to other software publishers and kick off another audit

DO research potential sales promotions, incentives, or goals that the account representative needs to meet. For instance, resolving an audit before the publisher's fiscal year-end; agreeing to replacing a competitor's technology in exchange for better terms; or providing an official corporate endorsement on the software publisher's promotional materials	DO NOT assume monetary penalties are the singular goal of the audit

A software license audit is never a welcome process, but being prepared for one is the crux of the responsibilities of an ITAM team. Invest the time now, when (hopefully) an audit is not on the horizon, to develop an Audit Response Playbook and support your ITAM team in learning what to expect during an audit. This preparation is guaranteed to pay off, even if you are lucky enough to avoid a license audit for years. Having your verifiably accurate ITAM data at the ready to face down any adversary is the entire point of ITAM and will add value in other areas of the business that you may not even expect.

CHAPTER 7

Building the Infrastructure for a Successful ITAM Program

A successful ITAM program often starts with a pile of data that's disorganized and difficult to parse. If you follow the *Pragmatic ITAM* methodology, it should end with a verifiably accurate, nearly complete picture of your computing environment and the exact data you need to share with internal teams as well as external auditors. The process is rarely a short road without hurdles, which means that before you dive in, you want to be sure you are starting with a strong foundation.

Launching a successful ITAM program means first investing in a foundational infrastructure that includes a conscientious ITAM team, a thoughtful training program, and policies and procedures that keep them focused on their goal.

Here's how to do it.

Building Your ITAM Team

We have covered the pieces of creating a functioning ITAM process. The processes are the engine of the *Pragmatic ITAM* methodology, but they don't run themselves. It takes skilled professionals with a special set of qualities to do the work required of an ITAM team.

If you want to be able to trust and rely on the data that your team returns, you want to make sure you trust and rely on the team themselves.

Qualities of a Good Asset Manager

If you have never hired an IT asset manager before, you should know that the majority of IT asset managers will learn on the job. That doesn't mean you won't be able to find anyone with relevant experience, but it does mean that during the hiring process, in some ways, you will be better off looking for immutable qualities that will make for a good asset manager rather than limiting your search to already developed skills.

A few qualities that I have found to be indispensable in an IT asset manager are:

Persistence

Uncovering and verifying all the data it takes for *Pragmatic ITAM* (or any ITAM methodology) to work effectively takes time and energy. The best IT asset managers will be people who do not tire of a task after one or twelve times and who are determined to always drill down to the right information instead of taking anything for granted.

Logical, Ordered Mind

While there is a bit of an art to effective ITAM, most of what an ITAM team does is follow concrete, inarguable data to logical conclusions. The path isn't always a straight line, which is why an appreciation of logic and a deep understanding of cause and effect are important traits for an IT asset manager.

Driven to Research

An ability to take on all kinds of research—from the in-depth technical explorations to the in-person questioning that's sometimes necessary—is critical for an IT asset manager. This should be the type of person who will keep following the threads the data gives them until they are satisfied they know the truth. They should also, ideally, be able to handle the truth[1].

---

[1] Here's where I'll note a related but still critical trait: what I call the "cast iron butt." There will be a lot of poring over difficult material, including software license agreements, in the asset manager role. Focusing on that type of thing for long stretches isn't for everyone, but it's important here.

I'm sorry, were you expecting a Jack Nicholson quote?

Thirst for Knowledge

Above all, an asset manager should always want to know more. Some of the most effective asset managers I have known have begun as auditors, where the whole job is uncovering data that may not be made readily available to them. An IT asset manager has to be willing to ask "why" something they find doesn't match up rather than accepting it as "good enough."

Core ITAM Team Roles

Many ITAM teams start off as one-person shows. In this case, you want to be sure that you have confidence in that one person to do the job right. As the program, and team, grows, you can look for people to fill these roles first:

- Data Analyst: Primarily concerned with moving data through the *Pragmatic ITAM* methodology. The Data Analyst is responsible for data entry and verification by way of the Discovery Tool Alignment reporting, verifying, and updating asset lifecycle flags by way of the ITAM Matrix reporting, and optimizing license position reporting by way of the DbIQ reporting. In larger organizations, Data Analysts can divide the work in ways that make sense: hardware versus software; end user versus server versus SaaS; and so on.
- ITAM Single Point of Contact (SPOC): Primarily concerned with providing expert information and education on ITAM concerns to fellow employees, software publisher account representatives, and license auditors. Project Managers turn to ITAM SPOCs with questions on hardware and software impacts from their programs. These are the people who warn the IT Finance group more software licenses will need to be purchased and track who will need to buy them. Of course, these are also the people who will play "point" when software audits occur. Larger organizations should divide these roles across software publishers, so the SPOCs can cultivate a deep knowledge of one specific publisher.

- Team Lead/Manager: As the team grows, someone will be spending more time managing human assets than IT assets. The Team Lead will be focused on creating and maintaining an environment where the rest of the team can do their work. They will be interviewing, hiring, and training team members as well as authoring, negotiating, and enforcing ITAM policies, standards, and procedures. And they will be the "face" of the ITAM team to the business leadership and other towers. Regardless of how big the team is, there can be only one of these.[2]

ITAM Team Training Basics

As we mentioned, a lot of learning for an asset manager happens on the job. As an IT leader, it's important that you have systems in place that facilitate this kind of learning and encourage learning that takes place outside of the office as well, particularly through community building in the ITAM world.

Have a SAM Tool in Place

One of the best ways to set a new asset manager up for success is to have a SAM tool in place already. Learning the ins and outs of that particular tool will go a long way toward setting your new hire up for success in the long term.

Implementing ITAM tooling while learning ITAM at the same time can be too much to take on. It's better to hire a consultant on a temporary basis to do the tooling implementation work. You only need that particular (and expensive) skillset for a short time and once everything is set up, your new asset manager can jump in and start learning. This type of strategy works well because you can leverage the

---

[2] "There can be only one!"—various, *Highlander* (1986). Please know, I do not endorse ritualized combat to resolve ITAM team disputes. Then again, any ITAM professional who walks in with Queen's "Princes of the Universe" is asking for a throwdown.

accrued knowledge of the consultant and only pay for it for a short time. Once you get the knowledge into your ITAM system, the system can tell you what the expert would have told you—without the hourly invoice.

It may also be tempting to simply rely on the SAM toolmaker themselves to install and set up your new system, but you need to be clear on where their responsibility ends. A SAM tool publisher will ensure that your software is installed to work as intended, but they will not be able to help you interpret any of the data it collects or even offer training on usage. It's a bit like buying a car. The dealer will be happy to show you all the bells and whistles on the lot and convince you it's the perfect car for you—but they're not going to teach you how to drive. This is why a third-party expert—a driving instructor for your SAM tool—can be invaluable during this process.

The ITAM Community

When something changes within the ITAM community, the first place an asset manager is likely to learn about the change is through another ITAM professional. That's why a new asset manager should do her best to integrate herself into the ITAM community as soon as possible. There are a few ways to do that.

- Join ITAM Associations
  The International Business Software Managers Association (IBSMA) and the International Association of IT Asset Management (IAITAM) are the two most relevant professional ITAM organizations. Both offer regular events for members as well as continuing education and certification courses in a range of ITAM specialties.
- Attend Events
  Events put on by ITAM groups like IBSMA and IAITAM are a great place to start, but other conferences across the country each year address topics both directly and tangentially related to ITAM. More importantly, these conferences give asset managers a chance to interface with other asset managers.

- Seek out Mentorships
  Mentorship from an experienced professional can be
  extremely worthwhile. Since there is so much on-the-job
  learning as an asset manager, having input from someone who
  has been there before can be invaluable. Third-party experts
  can be a valuable resource here, since they typically have years
  of experience and have held a variety of ITAM-related roles.

Policy, Standards, and Procedures

Once your ITAM team, whatever size it may be, is established, it's now
a matter of managing that team. No team will be able to achieve success
without clearly outlined policies, standards, and procedures.

Policies, standards, and procedures are a collection of documents
that describe how departments and teams are to execute the vision and
mission statements from corporate leaders.

The hierarchy of policies, standards, and procedures is as follows:

1. Policies: Demands and rules made to support and manifest the
   corporate vision.
2. Standards: Measure and guides to tell people whether they are
   correctly following the policy or not.
3. Procedures: Steps necessary to meet the demands of the policy within
   the confines of the standards.

On Wednesdays, we wear pink[3]

The aforementioned is a policy.

A standard would be what we mean by "Wednesdays." For instance, do
we only wear pink when at school? And only during the regular school year?

Another standard would be what constitutes "pink." Does it need to
be from a particular store or label? How much of an outfit must be pink
to count?

Finally, procedures would include how to obtain, prepare, and dress
in pink each Wednesday.

---

[3] *Mean Girls* (2004)

For an ITAM team to be effective, it will need policies, standards, *and* procedures to describe its place within the corporation, what is expected of it, and what authorities it has to enforce its rules.

There are too many variables to lay out the best policies, standards, and procedures that will work for every organization. This isn't a one-size-fits-all situation. However, there are common characteristics of effective ITAM policies (and standards and procedures) that I will outline so that you can review and revise yours as needed.

Policies, Standards, and Procedures for Pragmatic ITAM

This section will only deal with policies, standards, and procedures specific to ITAM that are designed to improve the ITAM Team's success. Other teams and departments might have their own policies, standards, and procedures that involve and/or impact the ITAM team, but what those look like are outside the scope of this book.

Common Policies Features for ITAM Teams

Feature 1: A declared IT tower is explicitly responsible and accountable for ITAM.

ITAM usually falls in one of three places, which will influence how it conducts business:

1. **IT Operations**—ergo, ITAM will have service delivery objectives. This is the most common setup for an ITAM team. These teams...
   ...are most comfortable dealing with service delivery CSFs and KPIs
   ...have the best access to CMDB asset and CI records, if not outright ownership
   ...will answer to the IT Chief of Operations (COO)
2. **IT Finance**—ergo, ITAM will have cost-reduction or spend-savings objectives. These ITAM teams are...
   ...most comfortable dealing with budgetary and cost-center reporting
   ...usually responsible for only the asset portion of the CMDB, or for their own Asset MDR that is separate from the CMDB
   ...will answer to the IT Budget/Finance liaison or CFO
3. **IT Security**—ergo, ITAM will have security and maintenance objectives. This setup is not as common, but its instances are growing. It's still unclear where the advantages of this type of setup lay, but in my

experience, it makes it somewhat easier and faster to get new ITAM programs started. These teams...

...will answer to the Chief Information Security Officer (CISO)

Each of these options has ITAM falling under the purview of another IT department, which means there's a risk that the needs/requirements of ITAM will get lost (because ITAM needs a little bit more than what those towers provide).[4]

You might be wondering: could ITAM exist as its own tower within the IT department?

Maybe. Possibly. It depends.

With the advent of the Chief Technology Officer (CTO), ITAM may be able to successfully exist as its own tower. The challenge here becomes defining the CTO role so that there is no overlap nor friction between the other IT towers. To set up an ITAM team this way, you will want to be able to definitively answer questions like:

- Does the CTO have authority over technology standards (which typically would lie with the COO or CIO)?
- Does the CTO have separate authority for the total cost of ownership, return on investment, run-rate charges, and so on, (which typically would lie with the IT Finance liaison)?
- For its part, the CISO role is so specialized that it's difficult to see where there would be a conflict with the CTO—but if you are planning an ITAM team that's structured this way, best check to make sure!

Ultimately, ITAM having its own tower under the CTO is the best of the imperfect options available. This setup gives the ITAM department every chance to get the resources and attention it needs.

Feature 2: ITAM's relationship with the IT department's vision and mission statements are clearly outlined.

There should be a bright line drawn from the ITAM team's activities to the IT department (or even better, Corporate) mission and vision statements.

"If there is no money, there is no mission"

---

[4] "Nobody puts Baby in a corner!"—Johnny Castle, *Dirty Dancing* (1987).

One former IT COO[5] I worked with offered this up as his ITAM team's mission statement. His vision was to leverage ITAM best business practices to reduce waste and improve IT run-rate for a hospital group. This rolled up into the healthcare institution's corporate goal of best-in-class patient health results.

By directly aligning the ITAM team's vision with the institution's corporate vision, it became much easier to justify the existence of (and any money spent on) the ITAM team, and it became easier to talk about the importance of ITAM to everyone in the organization. How? Because if ITAM doesn't do its job, you don't get paid!

Feature 3: ITAM policies, standards, and procedures are signed, dated, and reviewed on a regular basis.

Whoever represents the IT department to the business leadership should sign their name, certifying they approve of the language, date when the ITAM policies should be considered implemented, and include the date the documentation is regularly reviewed and updated. ITAM policies that are approved by leadership and regularly reviewed[6] offer more than just guidance, but can act as both a sword and a shield for when ITAM deals with software audits, license negotiations, and so on.

Good corporate practices should be to do this for all corporate policies, standards, and procedures. If your organization doesn't do this, you have bigger problems.

Common Standards of Measure

Standards of Measure, or simply standards, are the declaration of exactly how the success or failure of the policies are to be measured. There are a number of different independent standards that ITAM teams can draw from:

1. ISO 19770[7]
2. ITIL (really an ITSM standard)

---

[5] Matthew Eversole, circa 2016. I have witnesses.

[6] "And a mind needs books like a sword needs a whetstone, if it is to keep its edge. That's why I read so much." Tyrion Lannister, *A Game of Thrones*

[7] In one of those weird anticipatory coincidences, I started developing *Pragmatic ITAM* in earnest in 2015. I learned the details of the reworked ISO/IEC 19770:2017 standards in 2018. My notes aligned almost perfectly and convinced me I was on the right track!

3. IAITAM (provides a standards library via their certification program)
4. IT4IT
5. HiTRUST (really an ITSec standard)
6. Sarbanes-Oxley (really an ITFin standard)

Some ITAM teams will attempt to create their own standard. That is allowable, so long as the standards are consistent within themselves, within the standards from other teams in the corporation, and within the overall corporate standards.

Pragmatic ITAM should not be considered a standard, but a methodology that guides an ITAM team toward success as measured by their declared standards.

Suggested Features of ITAM Procedures

The old ITIL definition of a process is still the best:

> A structured set of activities designed to accomplish a specific objective, [which] takes one or more defined inputs and turns them into defined outputs.

ITIL tries to distinguish between processes and procedures but natural-speaking English treats the words as synonyms, and so will *Pragmatic ITAM*. Following is my preferred outline of features, but so long as these features are present in your procedure documents, the order itself doesn't really matter.[8]

---

[8] If you skip a step, you will know in a hurry, because you will have conversations like this one (South Park, "Gnomes" S2:17):
Gnome 1: Collecting underpants is just phase 1. Phase 1: collect underpants.
Kyle: Sooo, what's phase 2?
Gnome #1: [Stares blankly. Looks around, then calls out to other gnomes] Hey, what's phase 2?
Gnome #2: Phase 1: we collect underpants.
Gnome #1: Yeah yeah yeah, But what about phase 2?
Gnome #2: [Stares blankly, shrugs, then] Well, phase 3 is profit. Get it?
Stan: I still don't get it.
Gnome #2: [Walks up to large chart] Phase 1: collect underpants. Phase 2: ...
Phase 3: Profit.
Cartman: Oh, I get it.
Stan: No you don't!

Recommended Outline for *Pragmatic ITAM* Procedure Documents

1. **Purpose**: A brief paragraph describing what the process is and why it exists. Include the latest version number and version date from the Change Control section.
2. **Inputs**: A brief list of raw materials, information, or triggers that must be in place before work can begin.
3. **Outputs**: A brief list of completed materials, information, reports, and so on, generated by successfully executing the process. Critical Success Factors and Key Performance Indicators for measuring the effectiveness of the process should be detailed here.
4. **RACI Chart** (Responsible, Accountable, Consulted, and Informed): a chart listing the teams or roles participating in the work, and their contributions.

    a. Responsible—the team or role that will be starting the work and shepherding the work through completion
    b. Accountable—the team or role that will be ensuring the work is completed successfully and that the resulting outputs are acceptable for the stated purposes
    c. Consulted—a team or role that will be adding some sort of detail, approval, or coordination into the process (usually from another process they themselves are Responsible/ Accountable for)
    d. Informed—a team or role that will be taking some sort of detail, approval, or coordination away from the process (usually for another process they themselves are Responsible/ Accountable for)[9]

---

[9] Someone or some team needs to be Responsible for each discrete step of the work activities.

Usually, the group Responsible for the overall process is also Accountable for the results. Quality Control teams are about the only ones who are Accountable on their own, separate from the Responsible team. Look to the Standards documents if you need help or suggestions on what acceptable RACI Charts features are expected. Otherwise, there are plenty of resources outside this book.

5. **Activity**: A step-by-step outline of all the steps undertaken by various individuals or teams to complete the work.[10] If you have any diagrams or flowcharts to help visualize the process, these go here.

6. **Conclusion**: A brief paragraph containing any useful information about completing the process.

   Hyperlinks to other processes, exception processes, reports, service catalogs, and so on., will go here. If there are any separate instruction manuals for the process, make sure they are also mentioned, and a link to the document given.

7. **Change Control details**: Usually a chart detailing the procedure's version history (both major and minor), the changes made, the name of the individual making the changes, and the date the changes were made.

   Change Control is its own separate management discipline, so follow that group's rules for what does or does not necessitate a version change entry on this chart.

Recommended Procedures

While I can't and won't tell you exactly how your processes and procedures should look, I can recommend some of the most useful ones to have in place for your ITAM program.

Sample Operational Procedures

Procured

This procedure describes the steps necessary for creating CMDB/Asset MDR records for assets that are duly purchased, but not yet received, and setting their lifecycle flag to "Procured."

Inventoried

This procedure describes the steps necessary for receiving duly purchased assets, making them ready for use within the corporate environment, and

---

[10] The actual instructions on how to do each step belong in an Instruction Manual or Playbook, which is separate from this document.

updating the related CMDB/Asset MDR records to the "Inventoried" lifecycle state.

Installed

1. The DTA Report: This process describes the steps necessary for running the Discovery Tool Alignment (DTA) Report on a regular cycle (weekly, monthly, quarterly), identifying any inconsistencies and issues, informing the necessary parties to begin resolving any inconsistencies and issues, and delivering the completed report to the declared data customers.

2. The ITAM Matrix Report: This process describes the steps necessary for generating the ITAM Matrix Report on a regular cycle (weekly, monthly, quarterly), identifying any inconsistencies and issues with the asset lifecycle flags, informing the necessary parties to begin resolving any inconsistencies and issues, and delivering the completed report to the declared data customers.

3. The DbIQ Report: This process describes the steps necessary for generating the Database Integrity Quotient (DbIQ) Report on a regular cycle (weekly, monthly, quarterly), updating the Critical Field List with any new data attributes, identifying and explaining any issues and exceptions, and delivering the completed report to the declared data customers.

Recovered

This process describes the steps to be followed for determining if an asset pulled out of the computing environment has any more useful value. and updating the CMDB/Asset MDR record to the "Recovered" lifecycle state. The task then becomes to make the asset ready for redeployment back into the corporate computing environment.

Disposed

This process describes the steps to be followed for permanently removing assets from the corporate computing environment, updating the CMDB/Asset MDR asset lifecycle flag to "Disposed," and following any other related corporate policies and/or standards of care.

A Word on Exception Procedures

Adhere to the KISS principle[11]: Keep It Simple and Succinct. Good process design will describe the majority of the activities and have a limited number of steps to address infrequent but expected events where the process doesn't quite work.

Remember the old saw: "A chain is only as strong as its weakest link," and its corollary: "A process is only as good as its exceptions."[12]

---

[11] Not to be confused with the KISS mandate, which is "I wanna rock and roll all night, and party every day."

[12] Two notable exceptions do need to be discussed: Audit Response and Mergers/Acquisitions/Divestitures. We covered those in-depth in the previous chapter.

CHAPTER 8

The Future of ITAM

We can't know exactly what will come next for ITAM, but part of *Pragmatic ITAM* is looking toward new technologies and anticipating how the future will shape up for ITAM and the departments that rely on it.

We all know that the way things work today—scanning tools, license agreements, invasive audits—is not always going to be the way things work. Even now, we can look back just a handful of years and see how much has changed, with the Internet of Things (IoT) and external cloud services adding layers of complexity that we may not have expected and better automated processes working to better handle that complexity.

By looking toward the future, we can bolster support for our current ITAM programs and for the implementation of *Pragmatic ITAM* as a methodology. When we know where things are going, we can look at our current operations as stepping stones toward the next iteration of ITAM.

New developments will change the way we manage our assets. It's only a matter of time before some company (or companies) finds the right technological recipe to solve for the biggest issues in our current ITAM processes. The two advancements that I see as virtually inevitable are[1]:

1. Getting data to automatically flow into and out of the CMDB seamlessly (i.e., Digital Twin); and
2. Permanently solving the underlying problems within ITAM (i.e., blockchain).

---

[1] Get back to me in 20 years and we can decide together whether I should be declared Royal Smart Person or something less flattering. "Hey Smart Person, the King wants you!"—Sesame Street

The Digital Twin: CMDBs Fully Realized

Since their inception in the 1980s, CMDBs have earned a bad reputation of being too costly to maintain in both time and effort. This reputation is well deserved, especially in their early iterations. Early CMDBs focus on categorization of CIs, scattered static and dynamic information across asset records and CI records, and did not properly join and relate data from different internal tables to make timely and effective reports.

Fast forward to today, where the Internet of Things (IoT) is getting significant attention. IoT sees CPUs and Network Interface Cards (NICs) embedded in a number of mundane things—from light bulbs to conveyor belts, from thermostats to electric motors— that can communicate both what a thing is and also what it is doing with the other devices around it. Both sets of data are then leveraged to create a digital twin of the physical environment: an exact virtual model of the physical environment so accurate that changes made within the virtual space will confidently predict what will happen in the physical environment.

Imagine an assembly line with a number of IoT-enabled devices working together to produce a product. The industrial engineer could look at the digital twin of this line to see virtual product units being made at the exact same time as physical counterparts. Going further, the same engineer could test new configurations of the assembly line, find one that improves the efficiency of the entire process, and implement the change, certain that the actual results will match the virtual model.

In order for the digital twin to deserve this level of confidence, IoT-enabled devices need to deliver an inordinate amount of data about themselves, their status, and their work, and they need to do so nearly in real time. Further, the database rendering the depiction of the digital twin assembly line needs to be able to categorize the different types of data so that a clear and correct picture of the assembly line is generated.

This is exactly what the CMDB always promised and rarely delivered. Asset records hold the attributes about the device itself, and CIs describe the relationships between that device and others in the environment. When complete—or nearly complete—we should be able to have the same level of confidence that what we have is a clear picture of the computing environment.

This parallels what has happened with the Internet in general. Web 1.0 was merely one-way information transmission: think GeoCities, bulletin boards, and e-mail communication of old. Slow moving and time delayed, barely one step beyond its book publishing and letter writing analogs. Web 2.0 is Facebook, Fortnite, Minecraft,[2] and instant two-way information exchange encouraging both content creation and consumption. Instantaneous and obviously different to the communication methods before it.

Web 3.0 is shaping to be Machine Learning and Artificial Intelligence; where the system itself has enough data to identify patterns in usage and needs to anticipate bottlenecks and adjust accordingly. Remember Clippy of ye olde Office 97? The CMDB should pop up every once in a while and say "I noticed so-and-so has been assigned to this project—they will need a copy of Visio."[3]

Before a CMDB can act as a digital twin, someone needs to be the pathfinder, determining what feedback and standards must be implemented for maximum reliability. As the asset manager and service management department become more commoditized and less reliant on field interactions, the importance of creating a truly reliable CMDB becomes even greater. This reliability will manifest in huge cost savings as the most expensive parts (money and time) of the ITAM team's job can be those field interactions.

Blockchain

Much has been made of blockchain as the future of [*insert your preferred technology here*].[4] ITAM is no exception. It is more than likely that

---

[2] Minecraft is probably the best example of where the platform is taken in directions beyond anything the creators envisioned. Case in point: you can now play the video game Doom inside Minecraft. Think about that! A "build your own adventure" video game has the tools to allow players to build other video games and then play them within the original video game!!! Like the movie *Inception* (2010), but computers instead of dreams.

[3] Confession time: I always swapped out Clippy for the Einstein-inspired "Professor". It was the exact same dialog, but the animation delivered it more 'grandfatherly'.

[4] Simply google "Blockchain is a solution looking for a problem," and you will see dozens of articles with that title, all saying the same thing.

blockchain will have a major impact on how we implement and maintain ITAM practices in the coming years. Blockchain, in a way, is the natural extension of the idea of the Digital Twin.

Current SAM tools and methods are, at their core, inadequate. If existing methods were truly adequate, we wouldn't still be faced with regular audits and the rising threat of "shadow IT." The size and age of the current SAM tooling market is also an issue—aging systems are unable to keep up with the lightning-fast development of new technologies that present evolving challenges to asset managers and ITAM teams.

Yes, these issues extend to the *Pragmatic ITAM* methodology, which is imperfect itself.

But blockchain shows potential in solving two underlying issues of current SAM program implementations.

Why Do SAM Programs Keep Failing?

ITAM is a multibillion-dollar industry that has been around since the dawn of the computing age. While tools have evolved over these decades in an attempt to meet the changing needs of the software industry and its users, today's tools still largely fall flat.

What would it take to create a permanent solution to volume license agreements, software license audits, and so on? We keep telling people to "think outside the box," but we should be asking: "what's wrong with the box?"

The Double-Spend Conundrum

Hardware asset management is considered "easy" because it follows our innate sense of commerce.

A Simple Commerce Transaction

1. Buyer has money, wants goods; Seller has goods, wants money
2. Buyer gives money to Seller, Seller gives goods to Buyer
3. Buyer has goods, but no more money; Seller has money, but no longer has goods

Can a transaction like this be easily "hacked"?

Consider the "penny slug" gag from the early 20th century where a little kid would use a string tied around a coin to "hack" a vending machine. The coin would go into the slot up to the point where the machine would give up its candy, then the kid could pull the coin back out and use it again.[5]

So yes, there are examples of schemes that can "hack" a simple commerce transaction, but it's not that easy to pretend to give money to the seller, especially when buyer and seller are major corporations with a history of doing business, as is the case with many hardware transactions. And attempts to hack this kind of transaction present themselves pretty clearly as a deceptive, if not outright criminal, enterprise.

It's not as simple when we consider software asset management.

Software asset management is considered "difficult" because it can be effectively duplicated with little effort. Once you buy a single copy of a certain piece of software, nothing stops you from deploying it multiple times, with no loss of fidelity or functionality. This is where the idea of a "double spend" comes in: the money you would ordinarily spend on another copy of the software stays in your pocket.

Software publishers know how easy and tempting this kind of behavior is, which is exactly why they have created a number of mechanisms to prevent it:

License Keys: complicated codes that will unlock full functionality. Early on, these came in the guise of a physical dongle attached directly to the hardware. Today, alphanumeric codes designed to be so complicated that they defy easy memorization or sharing are more commonly used. And still, these keys are cracked, copied, and sold on the Dark Web.

Registration Accounts: usernames and passwords used to verify authorized usage.

With the rise of cloud computing, authorized accounts have become more useful because the bulk of software stays within the software

---

[5] My grandfather owned a coin-operated laundromat, and would mount a razor blade just inside the coin slot. The coin would fall past the blade, but if yanked back the blade would cut the string and end the gag!

publisher's controls. Still, registration accounts do not prevent unauthorized use. How many Netflix users share their information? And how can Netflix find illicit use within the proper use?

The nature of software has necessitated that publishers put in place these safeguards for their IP. These publisher protections, however, are not the cause of an ITAM team's struggles to maintain a handle on their software assets. Rather, the nature of how software is used, and by whom, within an organization creates a three-headed monster that puts up a constant fight with your ITAM warriors.

The Three-Headed Monster

The software asset management professional's problems are caused by three distinct groups, each with their own agenda:

1. Software Publishers
2. Corporate Customers
3. End Users

Software publishers are the holders of the intellectual property (IP) for the software. Creating, selling, maintaining, and supporting their software costs money. Not to mention, public companies have shareholders demanding dividends.

Corporate customers need to commoditize IT—make it better, faster, cheaper—to remain competitive. That means the corporate customer needs easy deployment, support and stability in order for their end users to be productive.

End users need software tools from the software publishers to create "the next big thing" for corporate customers and are also customers themselves of software publishers.

The common theme across all three groups? TRUST (or lack thereof). Software publishers do not trust corporate customers and end users not to abuse their IP. Corporate customers do not trust software publishers and end users not to put them at risk for financial and legal penalties. End users do not trust software publishers and corporate customers to provide cost-effective access to the tools needed to do their jobs.

Which brings us to the central challenge of software asset management: corporate SAM programs fail because they do not take each group's needs, demands and impact on each other into account.

How Can a SAM Tool Build Trust?

Trust but verify, as the old Russian proverb goes.[6] But how can a tool provide the kind of verification that earns the trust of everyone from the ITAM team to ITSec, to say nothing of external auditors? Earlier, we thoroughly explored why multiple data sources are necessary to provide this level of verifiable accuracy, so how can we now expect a single tool to provide it?

In the past, audits were the only option. We need a tool that presents all necessary aspects of a transaction to all parties. We need a tool with built-in protections from backdating and altering.

Enter blockchain.

What Is Blockchain?

Blockchain is an open, distributed ledger that can record transactions between two parties efficiently and in a verifiable and permanent way.[7]

Transactions, which are called blocks, are linked using a cryptographic hash of the previous blocks, a timestamp of the transaction, and the desired transactional data attributes.

Cryptographic hash is the result of a one-way algorithm that converts a record of any size into a series of alphanumeric characters of a fixed length. This method of encryption is considered "one-way" because the math to reverse the result to usable text is too difficult and time-consuming for current computing technology to manage.

Copies of the blockchain are stored on various computers within the blockchain network called "nodes." Nodes share the data attributes contained within the blockchain itself as well as the computational load of storing

---

[6] Ronald Reagan also found it handy when negotiating nuclear weapon limitation treaties.

[7] *The Truth About Blockchain,* Harvard Business Review, 2017

the files and instructions for the blockchain, authorizing and verifying new transactions and generating and confirming new encryption hashes. [8]

Benefits of a Blockchain System

Distributed

Copies of the blockchain are stored on various computers within the blockchain network called "nodes." Nodes share the data attributes contained within the blockchain itself as well as the computational load of storing the files and instructions for the blockchain, authorizing and verifying new transactions and generating and confirming new encryption hashes.

The distributed nature of blockchain means that every party participating in the blockchain (e.g., software publishers and corporate customers) have a copy of the blockchain on their own computer. Importantly, it isn't just a copy from a certain point in time, it is the same copy that everyone else has and it will update as the blockchain is updated with changes.

Anonymous

The identities of anyone (person or entity) using the blockchain can be hidden from the view of other participants without affecting the performance of the blockchain or its nodes. Furthermore, individual data attributes within the blockchain records can be restricted to a need-to-know basis from other participants if so desired. This is all initiated and controlled by the "smart contract" (see as follows). This anonymity would work in favor of an ITAM system since each user could include data on the blockchain that other users would not be able to access without compromising the overall security or integrity of the system.

Time Stamped

Not only are the date and time of the block's entry to the blockchain recorded, they are also used in the generation of the cryptographic hash of

---

[8] Cryptocurrency is an attempt to create a purely electronic form of money. Blockchain technology was proposed at the same time as cryptocurrency in order to electronically track the exchange of cryptocurrency for goods and services. Bitcoin (a specific "brand" of cryptocurrency and by far the most well-known) is to cash what blockchain is to a checking account statement.

the new record. This makes it nearly impossible for a bad actor to change data attributes after the new block is accepted and integrated into the ledger. Each time a change is made, the algorithm generates a brand new cryptographic hash with a new date and time tied to the event. All nodes will be alerted that something has changed. Postdating transactions or manipulating entries after they have been made becomes virtually impossible with this system.

In the case of a legitimate error, where new information is discovered and all parties in the blockchain agree it needs to be added, the chain forks: a new chain is created with records from the old chain up to where the new record needs to be added. The new record is added, the cryptographic hash is generated, verified, and confirmed by all nodes and parties of the blockchain. All the subsequent records are re-added as well, generating new hashes, new verifications and new confirmations. The old chain is then abandoned at the point of the fork and all new transactions are applied to the new chain.

Programmable

At its heart, a legal contract is a type of logical argument: If/when Person A takes an action, Person B responds with another action. Since blockchain is a computer program, it can follow logical rules to act and react to inputs and outputs. Blockchain can therefore be used to create a "smart contract" where the terms and conditions within the underpinning legal document can be automated.

Unanimous

All the network participants agree to the terms and conditions of the blockchain built into the smart contract. All the network participants have access to a node on the blockchain network, a copy of the blockchain, and a report on the verifications and approvals of new records on the blockchain added by other nodes.

Immutable

The blockchain is immutable thanks to the virtual impossibility of reversing the one-way algorithm to hide postdated changes to any one record and the distributed nodes that are constantly verifying and confirming the hash results of the existing records with one another.

Secure

For the same reasons that blockchain is immutable, it is secure. The one-way algorithm prevents postdated changes to any record, distributed nodes are constantly verifying and confirming new records on the chain and the encryption can be different for different parties with certain data restricted to a need-to-know basis.

What a SAM/Blockchain Solution Could Look Like

The features of blockchain just outlined give a good foundational picture of why Blockchain could have extremely useful applications in the field of software asset management. Here's one way this could shape up:

A smart contract is created to start the blockchain register and program the terms and conditions the Software Publisher and Corporate Customer agree to, like:

- How many installations of the software are allowed?
- Any geographic limitations? User limitations? Machine limitations?
- Can the Corporate Customer upgrade to newer versions when the Software Publisher releases updates and patches?
- How can the Corporate Customer request and pay for more installations when the need arises?

In short, anything that can be described within the written Terms and Conditions of a paper contract can be programmed into the smart contract.

The smart contract means that the Software Publisher and Corporate Customer are aware of any transactions (requests, distributions, consumptions, and recoveries) automatically. Both parties will have a node of their own with its own copy of the blockchain. Nodes work together to ensure the recorded transactions are accurately time-stamped, securely encrypted, and immutable. Both parties only share enough information about their activity to satisfy the smart contract—the "need to know."

The process could benefit end users as well, who are dissuaded from cutting corners when requesting installations and access. Does an end user really "need to know" software keys or permission settings to activate an installation when it is fully automated by the blockchain? A fully-automated software request process means the end user gets back to work sooner.

Any back channel installations are detected and reported to the nodes when software is activated, while security and encryption prevent reversing the blockchain itself for an end user (or nefarious party) to access the actual code. This fully-automated process means the end user gets back to work sooner while exposing the Corporate Customer to substantially less risk.

Potential Business Benefits of a Blockchain Implementation

Software Publishers, Corporate Customers and End Users could all see benefit to their business operations by implementing this type of technology.

Software Publishers

The nature of blockchain is such that the need for audits would be substantially reduced (if not eliminated entirely). What if software publishers could reallocate their audit resources toward something else? Audits are incredibly expensive for publishers, especially if a third-party is brought in to run them (think KPMG, Deloitte, PwC, E&Y). Those financial resources could be a boon to other departments within the publisher's corporate structure.

Audits are also expensive for publishers when it comes to their reputation. A particularly nasty audit can easily drive the Corporate Customer to a competitor. If audits were all but eliminated, it could mean a huge boost to customer retention and a related financial windfall for the publisher.

Corporate Customers

For the Corporate Customer's part, the massive reduction in audit risk could mean that the company can better budget for their IT costs. Audit penalties can be massively expensive, even forcing layoffs, eliminating employee perks and benefits, or denying bonuses to end users.

With the risk of an audit penalty gone, it could mean better allocation or reallocation or IT resources in such a way that end users can be more productive and IT systems can be more secure. For instance, not waiting for requested software to be approved, purchased, installed, and so on, increases time at task (and therefore productivity), while hiring more knowledgeable and better trained IT staff could make everything run more efficiently.

End Users

The benefits to end users are less directly fiscal but no less notable.

With blockchain implementation, end users could spend less time with the corporate bureaucracy of requesting software, waiting for it to be approved, and waiting for it to be installed, get more of the latest, greatest software tools they say they want and not worry about a layoff for something outside of their control, like a software license audit.

Outstanding Questions

A blockchain system could be beneficial on every level, but certain questions still need to be answered.

How do you close Corporate Customer's network to unlicensed installations?

A key piece to rebuilding trust between Corporate Customers and Software Publishers would be that all unlicensed software installation and usage will be detected and prevented. Solving this dilemma may require a number of different systems to work together that do not do so today: request systems, procurement systems, remote installation systems, local administration account controls, and so on. If this level of trust is established, end users benefit too. A network closed to unlicensed installations will be able to bring down many bureaucratic barriers to installing necessary software, making things a lot more efficient from the end user's perspective.

Will Software Publishers be willing to relinquish a revenue stream like audits?

Software Publishers are estimated to augment upwards of 40 percent of their sales revenue with audits—are they willing to walk away from this sizable amount of money? Of course, it's not free money for them. It costs a lot to hire auditors and chase that missing revenue, especially if litigation is necessary. If a Software Publisher could avoid those expenditures, even at the cost of the audit revenue stream, what else might they be able to spend their money on? It can really only go in two directions: either spent internally on the research and development of new software products and titles, or outwardly in the form of dividends to shareholders, either of which could be advantageous to the fiscal position of the company in the long run.

Should use license terms change to better leverage the advantages of blockchain?

Some Software Publishers contractually limit the frequency use rights can be transferred between end users and/or devices. What might work better for blockchain technology? Metered usage? Computational cycles? Demand metering? If end users agree to let their own devices act as blockchain nodes, would that impact the use license terms?[9] Mainframe licensing used to be based on how many "cycles" the program ran. That could make a comeback.

Where will the preferred solution come from: Software Publishers or a third party?

Would Corporate Customers trust a solution offered up by a historically bad actor from the Software Publisher space? If a third party, how will they convince Software Publishers and Corporate Customers to join?[10]

Blockchain is not a panacea for every challenge that faces a software asset manager, but the technology could address many problems that

---

[9] Until March 2020, the Search for Extraterrestrial Intelligence (SETI) offered a screensaver set to run when a computer was idle—it was analyzing radio waves looking for signs of intelligent life. Software publishers could use the computing power of end users to partially "pay for" the blockchain technology.

[10] One such third party may be NeoCor. I mention because they are the first-to-market with a software asset management solution built on blockchain to facilitate increased trust, efficiency and transparency, resulting in improved license tracking, faster transactions, and reduced risk through asset tracking. I believe in them enough to agree to sit on the CEO Advisory Board. I leave it to the reader to come to their own conclusion.

current tools do not. The reduction in audit risk alone makes it well worth investigating how blockchain technology could be effectively applied in the ITAM arena.

The future of ITAM is certainly not set in stone, but between blockchain and the digital twin, we can get a good picture of where it's headed. One way or another, new technologies will be widely adopted that allow for increased automation, improved data accuracy, and fewer external audits. As ITAM professionals, it is our job not to resist the changes that may make certain processes we're attached to obsolete, and rather to embrace the changes and find ways to work effectively within the parameters of these new developments.

CHAPTER 9

Conclusion

Although we have reached the last chapter of this book, your *Pragmatic ITAM* program is likely still in its nascent stages. This methodology can serve as guidance for your entire ITAM program, whether you add new hardware, buy new software, face an external audit, or change jobs or companies.

In the second half of this book, we've turned from the specifics of developing your ITAM program to maturity and toward leveraging your ITAM data for real business advantage. We've also looked toward the future, so that we can see how the practices put in place for an effective ITAM program can set you up for success even as technologies change.

Reviewing the Tenets of Pragmatic ITAM

Let's take a moment to review the central tenets of the *Pragmatic ITAM* methodology. This isn't the first time you have seen these, but they bear repeating.

1. Knowledge of the problem inherently changes the nature of the problem
   The more you learn about your computing environment, using a thorough discovery process, the better off you'll be. I've shown you how to effectively collect the data that will be most useful to share with stakeholders and that will save you in the event of a software license audit.

2. She with the best documentation wins
   Documentation is the point if you want your data to be verifiable. *Pragmatic ITAM* has shown you how to create processes and documentation that is easy to digest at a glance and, more importantly, impossible for auditors to argue with.

3. Work smarter, not harder

   Setting up a new *Pragmatic ITAM* program does involve some investment of time and resources. But once you have the foundation in place, you have an early warning system for anything that's threatening to go awry. The investment will pay off huge in even a single audit.

4. Trust, but verify

   Because verifiably accurate data is the goal of *Pragmatic ITAM,* it's never enough to take someone at their word. In this book, you've learned how to verify the data you're getting from multiple sources so that it's as accurate and up-to-date as possible.

5. Asset lifecycle management requires rigor

   Maintaining an accurate asset lifecycle means having a process in place to verify when any asset is moving from one stage to another. The CSFs and KPIs need to be crafted and reported to ensure process steps are not skipped and gaps in your understanding do not go undetected. It does take time, but that time investment will decrease the longer you maintain your *Pragmatic ITAM* practices.

6. Process is a means to an end, and is not an end itself

   Pragmatic ITAM does not prescribe a specific process for accomplishing your ITAM goals. Rather, I outline the pieces of the process that will be essential in establishing an effective, long-term ITAM program. It's up to you as a technology leader to find the exact process that gets you the data you need to keep things humming.

Review of Weaponizing Your ITAM During Mergers, Acquisitions, and Software License Audits

In this chapter, we reviewed why mergers, acquisitions, and divestitures are dangerous times for ITAM teams. Namely, these specific, disruptive business activities can often trigger an audit as software publishers aim to catch the business off guard.

Luckily, with the right preparation, your ITAM team can be well-prepared for the eventuality of an audit, even in the midst of M&A chaos.

Developing a response plan for a software license audit is, in many ways, the whole reason for investing in an ITAM program to begin with, so it should be fairly easy to see how this chapter relates back to our central tenets.

1. She with the best documentation wins
   Your *Pragmatic ITAM* documentation is critical in the audit process. Thorough documentation of your assets is the best weapon you can have against an adversarial auditor—and may indeed be the cause of great frustration on their part.
2. Process is a means to an end, not an end itself
   The *Pragmatic ITAM* process is designed to help you prepare for and conquer anything a software license audit can throw your way. Having beautifully organized, thorough data is nice, but weaponizing that data in the audit context is the whole point. *Pragmatic ITAM* is designed to be both a sword and a shield; defense and offense. You will save the company money and countless headaches if you leverage the *Pragmatic ITAM* process to prepare for the eventuality of an audit.

Review of Building the Infrastructure for a Successful ITAM Program

Before you can begin to build and optimize your ITAM program, you must have the right infrastructure in place. In this chapter, we examined the best practices for hiring, how to develop effective policies, standards and procedures, and some of the most common ways of organizing an ITAM team and program.

We can see how these *Pragmatic ITAM* tenets relate back to this chapter:

1. Work smarter, not harder
   The right personnel for an ITAM team (whether it's just one person or many) are those that thoroughly internalize this principle. They should be people that want to get to the root of a problem and find a verifiable answer as efficiently as possible, using all the tools at their disposal.
2. Asset lifecycle management requires rigor
   Developing policies, standards and procedures for your ITAM program means creating a repeatable process and guidelines for the whole program. Having this type of documentation in place in effect builds the foundation for the type of rigor necessary to maintain a functioning ITAM program.

Review of The Future of ITAM

Finally, we took a look at what the future of ITAM may hold. The predictions in this chapter are based on where technological capabilities stand now as well as decades of experience in this space. The two biggest takeaways from here are the idea of the digital twin as a replacement for a more traditional CMDB and the implications that blockchain technology is likely to have on ITAM programs.

Because we are literally predicting the future here, the tenets of *Pragmatic ITAM* apply a bit differently:

1. Knowledge of the problem inherently changes the nature of the problem
   As the digital twin comes to potentially replace the traditional CMDB, ITAM teams will have access to more knowledge about their computing environments than ever before. While this may mean that new issues arise, there will no longer be a problem with knowing with certainty what assets exist.
2. Trust but verify
   This tenet is perhaps best applied to the idea of blockchain technology. The beauty of implementing blockchain in an ITAM program is that it removes the idea of trust from the equation—all parties have all the information they need all the time and there is no possibility to alter, postdate, or otherwise mess with asset records. That's why it's the future.

What You Can Do Next

This is it. You've reached the end of this book, and not a monster to be found.[1] But this is just the beginning of your *Pragmatic ITAM* journey. How you have used this book since first picking it up has been dependent

---

[1] "The Monster at the End of This Book" by Jon Stone was the first book I remember ever reading. Family lore says I destroyed two copies during my early years. Another copy sits proudly in my library; a high school graduation gift from my grandmother.

on how mature your existing (or nonexistent) ITAM program was. Now, that's what will determine what you do next.

- Is it time to finally hire your first ITAM team member?
- Do you want to turn this guide over to your existing team and have them start implementing the *Pragmatic ITAM* methodology like, yesterday?
- Or are you ready to admit that you need help and are looking to work with a professional ITAM consultant to plan your next move?

Whichever it is, I hope you were able to find the resources you need to help you make that choice.

As with anything having to do with developing technology, ITAM as a field is constantly changing. This book should be a practical resource for years to come, but as new developments and new technology becomes available, I will be making updates, compiling research, and adding events to *www.PragmaticITAM.com* That is, until blockchain renders me, you, and everyone we know as completely obsolete.[2]

---

[2] I, for one, welcome our blockchain overlords. Apologies to *The Simpsons*.

Appendix A

Common ITAM "Critical Fields"

Following is a list of data record fields and inputs typically flagged as "critical" for *Pragmatic ITAM* purposes. This list includes the usual field name, notes about the information it carries, the usual source that can deliver the data to the CMDB or Asset MDR, and ease of automation. Ease of automation represents the following degrees of difficulty:

- Easy—should be expected as part of any action
- Medium—requires some procedural changes or manual research efforts
- Hard—no expectation of automated data entry

Do remember that each CMDB and Asset MDR manufacturer designed their tools slightly different. Field names can vary; fields can be in different tables. However, even if a critical field is missing from the pristine installation, most all modern CMDBs/Asset MDRs allow for customization to overcome the oversight.

#	Name	Notes	Source	Automation
1	Asset Name	NetBIOS or workgroup name	Discovery	Easy
2	Last logged in username	User name of most recent user to log in	Discovery	Easy
3	Last logged in date	Date stamp of most recent log in activity	Discovery	Easy
4	Top logged in username	User name with the most numerous logins	Discovery	Easy
5	Make	Manufacturer of the asset	Discovery	Easy
6	Model	Model name of the asset, set by the manufacturer	Discovery	Easy

7	Form factor	Design description that usually denotes the functionality of the device: laptop, desktop, server, mobile, etc.	Visual Inspection	Medium
8	Motherboard socket count	Total number of CPUs the installed motherboard can support	Discovery	Easy
9	Serial number	Unique identifier of the asset, set by the manufacturer	Discovery	Easy
10	Warranty date	Expiration date of manufacturer's included service support guarantees; also considered the end of the useful life of the asset	Research	Hard
11	Asset Tag	Unique identified of the asset, applied by the owner of the asset	Visual Inspection	Hard
12	Location	Description of the physical location where the device usually operations	Visual Inspection	Hard
13	Purchase order number	Record number of the purchase order from the procurement system	Procurement	Easy
14	Purchase Order Date	Date of purchase order issuance	Procurement	Easy
15	Cost center number	General ledger code number or budgeting code number describing source dollars for the duly-pur-chased asset	Procurement	Easy
16	Capital project number	General ledger code number or budgeting code number describing specific project budget for the duly-purchased asset	Procurement	Easy
17	Invoice Number	Record number of the invoice issued to the procurement system	Procurement	Easy
18	Invoice Number Date	Date of invoice issuance	Procurement	Easy
19	Order received date	Date when physical possession of assets is made	Inventory	Medium
20	Location received	Location where physically delivery of assets is made	Inventory	Medium
21	Purpose	Description of the business function of the device to determining 'rights of second use': production, test, development, loaner, backup, etc.	Visual Inspection	Medium
22	Installed Date	Date where device is connected to the computing environment to begin performing its designated function	Visual Inspection	Medium

23	Assigned To	User who is responsible to the work and condition of the asset in question	Visual Inspection	Medium
24	Assigned Date	Date where Assigned To user accepts responsibility for the device and its work	Visual Inspection	Medium
25	CPU Manufacturer	Manufacturer of the central processing unit of the asset itself	Discovery	Easy
26	CPU Model	Model name of the central processing unit within the asset itself	Discovery	Easy
27	CPU core count	Number of discreet processors on the CPU die	Discovery	Easy
28	Virtual or Physical device	Flag indicating if the operating system environment (OSE) is located on a discreet physical device, or hosted within a cluster or server farm.	Discovery	Easy
29	Host farm membership	The physical server(s) that provide the hardware base to host virtualized OSEs	Discovery	Easy
30	Last visual inspection date	Date stamp of most recent visual inspection activity	Visual Inspection	Hard
31	Last visual inspector	Name of individual who performed most recent visual inspection	Visual Inspection	Hard
32	Disposal date	Date stamp when organization is no longer in possession of the asset	Certificate of Disposal	Medium
33	Certificate of Disposal number	Document number showing custody of a particular asset has been transferred away from the organization	Certificate of Disposal	Medium
34	Subscription End Date	Date where subscription contracts are expected to expire	Research	Hard
35	Contract Number	Record number of the underpinning documentation and agreement paperwork within the contract management database	Procurement	Medium
36	Maintenance Right Quantities	Stores the number of use-rights covered by a maintenance or support agreement	Procurement	Easy
37	Use Right Quantities	Stores the number of use-rights duly purchased for that software or subscription	Procurement	Easy
38	Application ID	Internal identification number of each discreet software name, edition, version, and build to which discovered software relates over to	CMDB/ Asset MDR	Medium

39	General Ledger Number	Identification code relating back to the budgetary source for the purchase	Procurement	Easy
40	Installation Date	Date stamp marking when the asset was deployed to the computing environment	Discovery	Easy
41	Last Activation Date	Date stamp of most recently detect activity in the computing environment	Discovery	Medium
42	Average Use Time (foreground/ background)	Average measurement of the length of time the asset was actively used, and either directly or indirectly consuming CPU resources	Discovery	Medium
43	Installation Source	Origination of the software installation—package name, third-party, bring your own, etc.	CMDB/ Asset MDR	Medium
44	Publisher's/ Manufacturer's Sunset Date	Date where manufacturer's support for their product will terminate, or will become so prohibitively expensive, so that abandoning the current assets will be necessary	Research	Hard

Appendix B

Pragmatic ITAM Acronyms

AD	active directory
BYOD	bring your own device
CI	configuration item
CISO	Chief Information Security Officer
CMDB	configuration management database
CSF	critical success factor
CTO	Chief Technology Officer
DbIQ	database integrity quotient
DHCP	dynamic host configuration protocol
DNS	domain name system
EULA	end-user license agreement
FQDN	fully qualified domain name
HR	human resources
IAITAM	International Association of IT Asset Managers
IMoC	Install, Move, or Change
ISO/IEC	International Organization for Standardization/ International Electrotechnical Commission
IT	Information technology
ITAM	IT Asset Management
ITFin	IT Finance
ITIL	Information Technology Infrastructure Library
ITSec	IT Security
ITSM	IT Service Management
JML	join move leave
KPI	Key Performance Indicator
MA	master agreement
MDR	Managed Data Repository
OSE	Operating System Environments

PM	Project Manager
RACI	responsible, accountable, consulted, informed
SaaS	Software as a Service
SAM	software asset management
SCCM	system center configuration manager
SKU	stock-keeping unit
SME	subject matter expert
SPOC	Single Point of Contact
SSoT	Single Source of Truth
TCO	total cost of ownership
UUID	universally unique identifier
VAR	value-added reseller
VDI	Virtual Desktop Instances
VLA	volume license agreement

References

Ardolino, E. (Director). 1987. *Dirty Dancing* [Motion picture]. United States: Vestron Pictures.

Brooks, M. (Director). 1981. *History of the World*, Part 1 [Motion picture]. USA: 20th Century Fox.

Coppola, F.F. (Director). 1979. *Apocalypse Now* [Motion picture]. United Artists.

Deep Space Homer [Television series episode]. February 24, 1994. In *The Simpsons*.

Descartes, R. 2018. *Meditations on the First Philosophy*. Place of publication not identified: Simon & Brown.

Doom. [Video game]. 1993. id Software.

Fry, R. 2018. "Sleeping with the Enemy: How Major Audit Firms are Pursuing Their Own Clients." Available from https://cerno-ps.com/wp-content/uploads/2018/11/Cerno_White_Paper_-Sleeping-With-the-Enemy.pdf (accessed October 15, 2020).

Garner, B.A., and H.C. Black. 2019. *Black's Law Dictionary*. St. Paul, MN: Thomson Reuters.

Gilliam, T., and T. Jones. (Directors). 1975. *Monty Python and the Holy Grail* [Motion picture]. London: EMI Films.

Hein, R. February 10, 2014. "Tips to Get Ready for (or Possibly Avoid) Software Audits." Available from https://cio.com/article/2378880/tips-to-get-ready-for-or-possibly-avoid--software-audits.html

Hips Don't Lie [Recorded by S. Ripoll]. 2005. On *Oral Fixation*, Vol 2 [MP3]. Shakira.

Hughes, J. (Director). 1986. *Ferris Bueller's Day Off* [Motion picture]. Hollywood, CA: Paramount Pictures.

Iansiti, M., and K.R. Lakhani. August 21, 2019. "The Truth About Blockchain." Available from https://hbr.org/2017/01/the-truth-about-blockchain (accessed October 15, 2020)

International Standard: ISO/IEC 19770-1. 2017. Geneva, Switzerland: ISO/IEC.

Keillor, G. (Writer). 1974. *A Prairie Home Companion* [Radio series]. Minnesota Public Radio.

Lubin, A. (Director). 1941. *In the Navy* [Motion picture]. USA: Universal Pictures.

Martin, G.R. 2019. *A Game of Thrones*. New York, NY: Bantam Books.

Michaels, L. (Producer). 1975. *Saturday Night Live* [Television series]. NBC.

Minecraft. [Video game]. 2011. Mojang Studios.

Mitch Hedberg - Donut Joke [Video file]. October 16, 2019. https://youtu.be/xPq0-8dyl8I (accessed October 15, 2020).

Mulcahy, R. (Director). 1986. *Highlander* [Motion picture]. 20th Century Fox.

Nolan, C. (Director). 2010. *Inception* [Motion picture]. Warner Bros.

Pascal, B. 2018. *Pensees*. Place of publication not identified: Arcturus Publishing.

Plato, & Allan, D.J. 1965. *Republic*. London: Methuen.

Princes Of The Universe [Vinyl recording, Recorded by Queen]. March 1986. Capitol Records.

Reiner, R. (Director). 1987. *The Princess Bride* [Motion picture]. Santa Monica, CA: 20th Century Fox.

Reiner, R. (Director). 1992. *A Few Good Men* [Motion picture]. Columbia Pictures

Reinicke, C. June 21, 2018. "The Biggest Cybersecurity Risk to US Businesses is Employee Negligence, Study Says." Available from https://cnbc.com/2018/06/21/the-biggest-cybersecurity-risk-to-us-businesses-is-employee-negligence-study-says.html

Rickard, D. January 17, 2018. "The cost of 2017 Data Breaches." Available from https://csoonline.com/article/3249088/the-cost-of-2017-data-breaches.html (accessed October 15, 2020).

Rock and Roll All Nite [Vinyl recording, Recorded by KISS]. February 1975. Electric Lady Studios.

Scooby Doo, Where are You! [Television series]. 1969. CBS.

Sesame Street [Television series]. 1969. PBS.

Sesame Street. 1971. *The Monster at the End of this Book: Starring Furry old Grover*. Racine Wisconsin: Western Pub.

Shelton, R. (Director). 1988. *Bull Durham* [Motion picture]. United States: Orion Pictures.

Silver, J. (Producer), and The Wachowskis (Director). 1999. *The Matrix* [Motion picture]. Warner Bros.

Stone, M., and T. Parker. (Writers). December 16, 1998. Gnomes [Television series episode]. In *South Park*. Comedy Central.

Take This Job and Shove It [Vinyl recording, Recorded by J. Paycheck]. August 24, 1977. Billy Sherrill.

The Waiting [Vinyl recording, Recorded by T. Petty]. 1981.

Three Is a Magic Number [Television series episode]. 1973. In *Schoolhouse Rock!* ABC.

Tolkien, J.R. 2014. *The Fellowship of the Ring*. London, UK: HarperCollins.

Transparency Market Research. 2016. "IT Asset Management (ITAM) Software Market." Available from http://transparencymarketresearch.com/it-asset-management-itam-software-market.html (accessed October 15, 2020).

Waters, M. (Director). 2004. *Mean girls* [Motion picture]. Paramount Pictures.

Would I Lie to You? [Cassette, Recorded by A. Lennox & D. A. Stewart]. 1984. David A. Stewart.

About the Author

Jeremy L. Boerger started his career in Information Technology Asset Management (ITAM) fighting the Y2K Bug at the turn of the 21st Century. Since then, he has helped companies in manufacturing, healthcare, banking, and service industries build and rehabilitate successful hardware and software asset management (SAM) practices. These experiences prompted him to create the *Pragmatic ITAM* method, which directly addresses and permanently resolves the fundamental flaws in current ITAM and SAM implementations. He also tours the country, speaking at numerous conventions and symposiums throughout the year. In 2016 he founded Boerger Consulting, LLC, to better help business leaders and decision makers fully realize the promises a properly-functioning ITAM and SAM programs can deliver. In his off hours, you will find him at home in Cincinnati, Ohio, with his wife and family.

Index

OTHER TITLES IN THE INFORMATION SYSTEMS COLLECTION

Daniel Power, University of Northern Iowa, Editor

- *Computers and Information Processing for Business* by Sergio Ribeiro
- *Mastering the 7 Dimensions of Business-Technology Alignment* by Ashish Pachory
- *Aligning Technology with Business for Digital Transformation* by Ashish Pachory
- *Creating a Culture for Information Systems Success, Second Edition* by Zakariya Belkhamza
- *Business Continuity in a Cyber World* by David Sutton
- *Data-Based Decision Making and Digital Transformation* by Daniel J. Power and Ciara Heavin
- *Computer Support for Successful Project Management* by Ulhas Samant
- *Successful ERP Systems* by Jack G. Nestell and David L. Olson
- *Decision Support, Analytics, and Business Intelligence, Third Edition* by Daniel J. Power and Ciara Heavin
- *Building Successful Information Systems* by Michael Savoie
- *Computer Support for Successful Project Management* by Ulhas Samant
- *Information Technology Security Fundamentals* by Glen Sagers and Bryan Hosack
- *Creating a Culture for Information Systems Success* by Zakariya Belkhamza
- *Decision Support, Analytics, and Business Intelligence* by Daniel Power
- *Building Successful Information Systems* by Michael Savoie

Announcing the Business Expert Press Digital Library

Concise e-books business students need for classroom and research

This book can also be purchased in an e-book collection by your library as

- a one-time purchase,
- that is owned forever,
- allows for simultaneous readers,
- has no restrictions on printing, and
- can be downloaded as PDFs from within the library community.

Our digital library collections are a great solution to beat the rising cost of textbooks. E-books can be loaded into their course management systems or onto students' e-book readers. The **Business Expert Press** digital libraries are very affordable, with no obligation to buy in future years. For more information, please visit **www.businessexpertpress.com/librarians**. To set up a trial in the United States, please email **sales@businessexpertpress.com**.

CPSIA information can be obtained
at www.ICGtesting.com
Printed in the USA
BVHW092301210322
632033BV00010B/118

9 781637 420140